Enslaved Archives

ENSLAVED ARCHIVES

Slavery, Law, and the

Production of the Past

MARIA R. MONTALVO

JOHNS HOPKINS UNIVERSITY PRESS | *Baltimore*

Johns Hopkins University Press
2715 North Charles Street
Baltimore, Maryland 21218
www.press.jhu.edu

Library of Congress Cataloging-in-Publication Data

Names: Montalvo, Maria R., 1989– author.
Title: Enslaved archives : slavery, law, and the production of the past /
Maria R. Montalvo.
Description: Baltimore : Johns Hopkins University Press, 2024. | Includes
bibliographical references and index.
Identifiers: LCCN 2023049540 | ISBN 9781421449463 (hardcover) |
ISBN 9781421449470 (ebook) | ISBN 9781421449500 (ebook other)
Subjects: LCSH: Slavery—Law and legislation—United States—History—
19th century. | Slavery—Moral and ethical aspects—United States—History—
19th century.
Classification: LCC KF4545.S5 M49 2024 | DDC 342.7308/7—dc23/eng/20240116
LC record available at https://lccn.loc.gov/2023049540

A catalog record for this book is available from the British Library.

This book is freely available in an open access edition thanks to TOME (Toward an
Open Monograph Ecosystem)—a collaboration of the Association of American
Universities, the Association of University Presses, and the Association of Research
Libraries—and the generous support of Emory University and the Andrew W. Mellon
Foundation. Learn more at the TOME website, available at openmonographs.org.

*Special discounts are available for bulk purchases of this book. For more information,
please contact Special Sales at specialsales@jh.edu.*

There is no telling this story—
In its potent ability to decree what is is not, as in a
human ceasing to be and becoming an object, a thing
or chattel, the law approaches the realm of magic
and religion. The conversion of human into chattel
becomes an act of transubstantiation the equal of the
metamorphosis of the eucharistic bread and wine into
the body and blood of Christ. Like a magic wand the
law erases all ties—linguistic, societal, cultural,
familial, parental, and spiritual; it strips the African
down to the basic common denominator of man,
woman, or child, albeit sometimes meagre. Without
a history, name, or culture. In life but without life.
Without life in life—with a story that cannot but
must be told.

—M. NOURBESE PHILIP, *Zong!*

CONTENTS

ACKNOWLEDGMENTS

I did not just write this book with the Southern Outrages, I also wrote it for them. Since May 2020, we have convened on Thursday nights to think, laugh, and learn together. Samuel Abramson, Lauren Brand, D. Andrew Johnson, Sheridan Wright Kennedy, Keith McCall, David Ponton, Whitney Nell Stewart, Edward Valentin Jr., Ben Wright, and Miller Shores Wright read and critiqued most every word of this book with the kind of love, empathy, and support that most scholars only dream of. Thank y'all for everything. More Thursdays. More Outrage. More life.

I am especially indebted to Andrew Johnson, who helped me develop this project in text messages, conversations, and writing retreats. Since graduate school, our friendship has evolved into my favorite place to practice history. Andrew, I consider it a privilege to call you my Write or Die, and I look forward to learning with and from you for years to come.

I began working on this project when I was a graduate student at Rice University. I could not have started or finished this book without the mentorship and guidance of W. Caleb McDaniel, Jim Sidbury, Edward Cox, Allen J. Matusow, Alida C. Metcalf, Fay Yarbrough, Lora Wildenthal, Peter C. Caldwell, Moramay López-Alonso, John Boles, Jacqueline Jones, Jeff Forret, and Jennifer Bratter.

I started transforming my studies into a book when I was the Bonquois Postdoctoral Fellow in Women's History in the Gulf South at the Newcomb College Institute of Tulane University. I am sincerely grateful to the faculty and staff at Newcomb, as their support was instrumental in my development as a historian and a scholar.

I am similarly grateful for the support of the Gilder Lehrman Institute of American History, the Economic History Association, the American Historical Association, the University of North Carolina's Southern Historical Collection, the Humanities Research Center at Rice University, the American Society for Legal History, Duke University's John Hope Franklin Research Center, and the Ethel and Herman L. Midlo Center for New Orleans Studies at the University of New Orleans. Archivists at the New Orleans Public Library and the New Orleans Notarial Archives offered vital insights and support that made examining thousands of sets of records possible and enjoyable.

It is not lost on me that I had the time and resources necessary to complete this project because I am an assistant professor of history at Emory University. From the moment I set foot on campus, the faculty, staff, and administration at Emory have made sure I was supported, in every sense of the word. I consider getting to teach, research, and learn at Emory the greatest privilege of my professional life. I am especially grateful to Patrick N. Allitt, Erica Bruchko, Adriana Chira, Joseph Crespino, Astrid M. Eckert, Becky Herring, Jazlyn Ann Jones, Daniel LaChance, Jeffrey Lesser, Judith A. Miller, Matthew J. Payne, Jonathan Prude, Thomas D. Rogers, Allison C. Rollins, Walter C. Rucker, Ellie R. Schainker, Kylie Smith, Sharon T. Strocchia, Allen E. Tullos, Brian Vick, Jason Morgan Ward, Katie B. Wilson, Yanna Yannakakis, and last but never least, the members of the Wolf Pack, Carl Suddler and Chris Suh.

Tiera Ndlovu worked to fact check my freedom suit data amidst the beginnings of a global pandemic. I have learned so much from getting to know her and reading her work. Thank you for helping me move forward with this project. Hannah Charak picked up where Tiera left off, critiquing the entire manuscript and tracking down sources that had long eluded me. There are few historians I trust more than Hannah. Wherever she decides to channel her considerable, dogged research skills in the future, I am certain this world will be better for it.

As I worked to complete this project, I had the pleasure of learning from and receiving feedback from some very generous folks, including Caitlin Rosenthal, Alejandra Dubcovsky, Stephanie E. Jones Rogers,

Alexandra J. Finley, Marisa J. Fuentes, and Amrita Chakrabarti Myers. I also had the opportunity to workshop parts of the book with several groups, including the Southern Historical Association's Junior Scholars Workshop, the "Visions of Slavery: Histories, Memories, and Mobilizations of Unfreedom in the Black Atlantic" Mellon Sawyer Seminar, and the "Race and Slavery Working Group." I am grateful to the participants and organizers for including me and giving me the opportunity to refine my work.

In the process of writing this book, I had the opportunity to conduct a manuscript workshop. Ariela Gross, Jessica Marie Johnson, Joshua Rothman, Daniel LaChance, Judith Miller, Jonathan Prude, Tom Rogers, Carl Suddler, and Chris Suh graciously agreed to participate, and each provided invaluable feedback that was instrumental in my getting this thing across the finish line. I learned so much from working with y'all, I am sincerely grateful for your time and efforts, and I look forward to returning the favor someday.

It has been my good fortune to have friends and family whose care and encouragement has never wavered. I am exceedingly grateful for Nora Venegas, Joe Galindo, Jorge Galindo, Sarah Peña, Nora Montalvo-Liendo, Teri Montalvo, Tony J. Carrizales, Diego Medellin, Guadalupe García, Ana Goñi-Lessan, LaNita Gregory Campbell, Tara Johnson, Ruby Johnson, Cole Johnson, Brad Rothwell, Peggy Rothwell, and Chris Rothwell. Thank you to the Primas, Lily, Jolene, and Tito, for their ongoing, insatiable commitment to distraction and chaos. My brothers and parents, Rene P. Montalvo and Norma Venegas Montalvo, have been a source of unyielding support and love. Thank y'all for believing in me.

Finally, I never miss a chance to call my friendship with William Ryan Rothwell the blessing of my life. Without him, this book and I would be incomplete. Bill, thank you for being my best friend, and thank you for letting me be yours.

Enslaved Archives

Introduction

On John

History is the fruit of power, but power itself is never
so transparent that its analysis becomes superfluous.
The ultimate mark of power may be its invisibility; the
ultimate challenge, the exposition of its roots.

—MICHEL-ROLPH TROUILLOT, *Silencing the Past*

TO STUDY ENSLAVED PEOPLE is to encounter enslavers' power at most
every turn. You cannot escape it. You cannot destroy it. All you can do
is decide whose story is most important to the history you wish to write
and then do everything you can to write it. This is not to say that power,
or its role in producing the materials we rely on in our attempt to reconstruct the past, is always easy to see. Working to expose that power is
an essential, important exercise not only in writing histories of enslaved
and disenfranchised people but also in undermining the stories that their
enslavers and oppressors wanted told.[1]

When I started working with the records at the center of this book—
antebellum New Orleans court records from civil suits that centered
on enslaved individuals—I thought I had struck gold. Here were lawsuits, hundreds of them, in which enslavers, lawyers, and witnesses told
and documented stories about enslaved people. Scholars of slavery often
lament the absence of such people from the written record, but here were
extensive biographical details, the likes of which I have never encountered before or since. And here was an opportunity to write a history
from the courtroom that centered those unable to speak and have their
words documented within its four walls. I was right, but I was also
wrong.

I got so lost in the stories that for a time, I failed to remember who was doing the telling and to what end. I wrote paragraphs and papers in which I recounted what transpired in lawsuits as if I were writing a history of enslaved people's lived experiences. I was not. I was simply summarizing what enslavers, people with immense social power, said in court about people with none. Only after I started learning from scholars who critically consider the nature of the written archive did I begin to realize that if I did not ask questions about the production of these records—and about what it meant to be enslaved in a world where, sometimes, your history was worth recording—all I would be doing was rewriting the stories that enslavers wanted told. This book is my attempt to do something different.[2]

Between 1804 and 1862, at least 135,000 people were sold in New Orleans.[3] On February 4, 1858, John became one of them. I don't know where he was born. I can't tell you where he died. I don't know where his people were, what he dreamed about, or where he most wanted to be. Indeed, much of what I can reasonably conclude about John comes from my reading of a single contract. I can tell you that on that February day, a slave trader named Bernard Kendig sold John to Thomas Gatlin, an Arkansas cotton planter. I can also tell you that five words, "John aged about fourteen years," are all that remains of him in the written record. The question "Who is John?" is impossible to answer. And yet, asking questions about people, like John, who briefly appear and disappear in written records can still help us learn something about enslaved people's lives and the business that shaped them.[4]

What we can and cannot learn about John is emblematic of how scholars of slavery in the nineteenth-century United States typically find enslaved people in the written record: a name—typically only a first name—an age, a sex, and a price. "The medium of biography," Annette Gordon-Reed writes, "so effective in conveying information about times gone by, and perhaps the most accessible form of historical writing, is problematic in the context of slavery."[5] It is problematic because, for those of us invested in learning about the lives of enslaved individuals, we are so often at the mercy of what their enslavers wrote down about them. Indeed, the sources we rely on, first, were usually not written by enslaved people, and second, were typically written at moments when the enslaved were being treated as property (bought, sold, mortgaged, and so on). Thus, the nature of the sources that historians of enslaved people work with are such that we are not only largely dependent on an archive created by enslavers, but we also rely on an archive that is lacking in much biographical information about specific enslaved individuals.

Enslaved Archives narrows in on the creation and preservation of legal records as a means of exploring the relationship between historical production and the commodification of enslaved human beings.[6] The book exposes how enslavers relied on their ability to produce written records to turn people into property. It examines moments when, for antebellum enslavers, information about the people they enslaved became worth recording. And it demonstrates that commodifying enslaved human beings was a process of not only exploiting someone's body and labor over the course of a lifetime but also defining what others could learn about an enslaved individual at a particular moment and over time.[7] In "Venus in Two Acts," Saidiya Hartman writes that "given the condition in which we find them [enslaved people], the only certainty is that we will lose them again, that they will expire or elude our grasp or collapse under the pressure of inquiry."[8] These losses, which are as certain in the nineteenth-century United States as they were in the era of the transatlantic slave trade, are important and worthy of our study and attention. The losing—how and why enslavers worked to make it happen, what it meant for enslaved people in life, and what it means for those of us who wish to learn about the lives of enslaved individuals now—is the subject of this book.

Legal records were at the heart of the business of slavery, and they are at the center of this book.[9] *Enslaved Archives* draws on my analysis of more than 18,000 sets of civil court records from antebellum New Orleans, including each of the extant 17,006 civil suits tried before the Orleans Parish Court between 1813 and 1846—records that are housed at the New Orleans Public Library's City Archives and Special Collections. Between 1813 and 1846, Orleans Parish was home to two courts that oversaw civil disputes: the Orleans Parish Court and the First District Court of Louisiana. These courts presided over countless lawsuits that centered on the workings of North America's largest slave market. The Orleans Parish Court's records have been microfilmed in their entirety, and the First District Court's records have been microfilmed selectively, according to which records the Genealogical Society of Utah deemed "genealogically significant."[10] When I started this project, I aimed to find enslaved people in these records, but there was no subject index of the Orleans Parish Court or First District Court records—meaning, there was no way to know how to find exactly the type of lawsuit I was looking for. I thus decided to create a subject index of the Orleans Parish Court's records, a database that lists the subject of each existing lawsuit tried before the court. In my search for enslaved individuals, I also created two databases based on my analysis: the first includes each of the slave-centered warranty disputes tried before the court, and the second includes each of the freedom suits tried before the court. These databases make up the central source base for this project and are available on the website of the New Orleans Public Library's City Archives and Special Collections.

When enslavers set foot inside New Orleans's courtrooms—to contest sales, claim warranties, and protect their investments in the people they enslaved—they and their attorneys became historians of the enslaved; the enslavers and their attorneys sought out written evidence; interrogated enslaved individuals, imposing invasive physical examinations; and worked to locate free individuals who could corroborate their claims about the past. In reconstructing an enslaved person's history in court, enslavers also revealed other moments when controlling information about specific enslaved individuals was an essential part of effectively exploiting one's enslaved property. I thus read court records for practices and processes of commodification as well as traces of the lives and voices of the enslaved. What can I know about this person? And why can't I know more? Asking and working to answer these questions about specific enslaved people reveals how these were also important questions for antebellum enslavers, who were invested in controlling what information about the people they enslaved was and would be available. That is not to say that enslavers were writing for historians; they were not. They were—in the interest of incentivizing sales, securing advantageous terms, and managing risk—writing for one another, the state, and themselves. Determining how and why can help us use these records to write histories of enslaved individuals. It can also help us understand not only the relationship between historical production and commodification but also the nature and limitations of capitalism, the law, and enslavers' power in the antebellum United States.[11]

I have chosen to focus on warranty disputes and freedom suits because these lawsuits centered individual enslaved people's histories. Warranty disputes arose because throughout the antebellum period, Louisiana maintained a set of warranty regulations that were unique to the state called redhibition laws. These laws regulated the exchange of information between slave buyers and sellers as well as defined the terms under which a dissatisfied buyer could have a sale canceled. While we know that not everything in the marketplace is done according to the letter of the law, I demonstrate that enslavers who did business in Louisiana and elsewhere recognized the state's peculiar market regulations as a tool of the trade, used not only to negotiate sales but also to define what information was preserved in contracts over time. Taking a closer look at how and to what end they did so reveals some of the moments when and strategies through which enslavers used paper and archives to control what others could and would learn about the people they bought, sold, and owned. Contracts and court records from redhibition suits thus show us how enslavers used these regulations to make decisions in the market and at the level of the page.[12] These records also allow us brief glimpses of the lives of specific enslaved individuals. I aim to use these sources, not to simply summarize what these records say about enslaved people, but to explore: first, the moments when information about enslaved individuals became worth recording and controlling; second, what it meant to be at once enslaved and the subject of enslavers' historical machinations; and finally, the long-term consequences for scholars invested in historicizing enslaved people.

Court records from freedom suits tried in antebellum New Orleans provide another significant window into the processes through which human beings were transformed into valuable commodities. While scholars have often used records from freedom suits to study the history of freedom, race, slavery, and the law, historians of slavery and capitalism have yet to consider what they reveal about the process of making people into products. By taking a closer look, first, at how enslavers created and manipulated evidence of enslavement to enslave free people of color and, second, at the obstacles that enslaved plaintiffs encountered when attempting to prove that they were entitled to their freedom, *Enslaved Archives* illuminates the extent of the power that enslavers enjoyed in their ability to create evidence that made nonwhite individuals legible as enslaved property.[13]

New Orleans is a looking glass. Its unique legal regime allows us to glimpse the aspirations, priorities, and strategies of enslavers from across the slaveholding United States. What could and did happen in New Orleans is an important part of this story, but this book stands to teach us more than something about that city. This is a book about American enslavers, their violent work, and its consequences. It is filtered through the lens of New Orleans's courtrooms, which I understand as the arms of an institution that shaped what was possible and profitable in North America's largest slave market and elsewhere. Because there were moments when, to get what they wanted in court, enslavers and their attorneys had to construct historical narratives that extended years into an enslaved person's past, court records sometimes allow us to see the disparate paths that enslavers and the enslaved took to the Crescent City, providing important insight into what drew enslavers to New Orleans as well as the workings of the domestic slave trade. Court records also allow us to come to the conclusion that slavery was a historical enterprise, because in order to hold people as property, a human being's past had to be curated and controlled.[14]

This book consists of five chapters. Each chapter focuses on a specific enslaved individual. I have chosen this approach, first, because the historical and archival maneuverings of enslavers are most visible at the level of the individual, and second, because I am primarily interested in the relationship between biography and power. Focusing on what we can and cannot learn about specific enslaved individuals thus allows me to reflect on the historical production of biographical information and the lingering consequences for those of us who wish to learn about the lives of enslaved individuals.

Now, for a bit on what I hope you take away from each chapter: Chapter 1 is and is not about an enslaved child named John, the same John I mentioned at the start of this introduction. In the interest of historicizing John, a person whom I encounter in a single contract, I explore and trace the production of said contract, illuminating not only how important these records were to enslavers but also how enslavers used them to define what others would and could learn about specific enslaved individuals. In this way, this chapter links the production of property to the production of the past, as well as demonstrating how and why we find and lose so many enslaved people in acts of sale.

Chapter 2 is about Isaac Wright, a free person of color who was kidnapped and enslaved. In Wright's experiences, which we encounter through court records and newspaper accounts, we find a part of John's story that we can never access via contracts: namely, that enslavers' interest in controlling the past created circumstances wherein enslaved people were expected to recite and repeat history. In Wright's terrible, terrifying experiences, we see that time and time again, his ability to reconstruct his own past was a central part of his enslavement, thus bringing to light the historical and intellectual labor that enslaved people like John were expected to perform.

Chapter 3 is about Jack Smith, an enslaved man who found himself at the center of a warranty dispute during the last months of his life. In this chapter, I grapple with court records from a dispute wherein enslavers and witnesses were invested in recounting Smith's history, asking what we can learn about Smith's life and the circumstances that shaped it. In working to reconstruct the last year of Jack Smith's life, we see a world where enslaved people were central and essential to enslavers' efforts to reconstruct the past and transcend the limits of the written archive. Also, crucially, this chapter demonstrates that enslaved people were not only the subjects of enslavers' lawsuits but also, sometimes, active participants in their making.

Chapter 4 turns from warranty disputes to freedom suits, lawsuits that I believe have something to teach us about how enslavers used paper and archives to transform free individuals into slaves. This chapter is about Betsey, a free woman of color who was kidnapped and enslaved in antebellum New Orleans, where she subsequently sued her enslaver for freedom. Using court records to trace Betsey's path through New Orleans's court system, this chapter examines the terrifying power of the slavers' archive, which could be used to erase, obscure, and nullify history in the interest of commodifying free people of color.

Finally, chapter 5 is about Sarah Ann Connor, an enslaved woman who won her freedom via sale and in a New Orleans courtroom. After establishing her freedom, Connor became an enslaver. In her efforts to participate in the business of slavery, we find the racial and gendered limits of the slavers' archive. Indeed, while Connor was able to buy and sell enslaved people, create documents, and enter courtrooms to protect her investments in enslaved property, time and time again she ran up against the limits of a business that was not built to work for her. This chapter thus intervenes in a historiography that has largely defined the business of slavery according to the legal and financial maneuverings of white men, demonstrating that archival power, participation in the business of slavery, and the ability to exploit its greatest, most terrible possibilities were most always tied to whiteness.

In centering individual lives alongside the production of the written records that define what we can and cannot learn about them, I aim to illuminate how and to what end enslavers endeavored to control information about the people they owned, how their efforts yielded important consequences for those they enslaved, and what that means for those of us who wish to learn about the past. Because each chapter focuses on a single individual, no two chapters bookend neatly with one another, and each varies in length and in level of detail. They move forward and backward in time, reflecting the nature of the written archive, which frequently stops and starts, sometimes revealing individuals and making them disappear in a single page. I am thus primarily concerned with the consistent, deliberate strategies and institutions that enslavers used to control not only the lives of the enslaved but also what parts of their lives we can access from when and where we are now.

Enslavement always involved a claim on a human being's past. When John's enslavers penned the contract that marks his entrance and exit from the written record, they also made a claim about his history and his future: specifically, that he had previously been and therefore could continue to be enslaved. What can we learn about enslaved individuals from the evidence that facilitated their enslavement? What do the possibilities and limits of these sources tell us about enslaved people's lives and the circumstances that shaped them? I believe we must study the historical and enduring significance of enslavers' power if we hope to learn anything about the enslaved from these records.

I will never be able to answer every question I have about the enslaved and vulnerable people at the center of this book. And yet, each of our unanswered questions can tell us something important about them and the world as it then was—but only if we do the work of not just acknowledging our unanswerable questions but also identifying and undermining the systems of violence and oppression that made these questions impossible to answer.

CHAPTER I

John and a Bill of Sale

Creating Property in Antebellum New Orleans

How might we take this evidence and venture toward
another mode of human being—so that when we encounter the lists, the ledgers, the commodities of slavery, we
notice that our collective unbearable past, which is
unrepresentable except for the archival mechanics that
usher in blackness vis-à-vis violence, is about something
else altogether.

—KATHERINE MCKITTRICK, "Mathematics of Black Life"

ON FEBRUARY 4, 1858, Thomas Gatlin and Bernard Kendig made a deal.
In exchange for $2,200 cash, Kendig would sell Gatlin an enslaved man
named Jim Gall and a child named John. After agreeing on a price and
a warranty, Gatlin and Kendig argued over whether they would create
a bill of sale. While Gatlin insisted they put the terms of their deal to
paper, Kendig initially refused, as he thought an act of sale "was too
binding." Finally, after some discussion, Kendig relented, and he and
two witnesses signed a contract.[1]

The document that Kendig signed bears no mark of his hesitation.
When read in isolation, it almost seems inevitable. There was a sale, so
of course there is a contract. But because this particular act of sale was
used as evidence in a lawsuit, and because a lawyer asked a witness to
describe the circumstances surrounding this transaction, we know that
its production was not inevitable. It was uncertain, even contested, until
Bernard Kendig and Thomas Gatlin decided to create it.

Contracts tend to hide more than they reveal. In addition to providing little insight into its production, the contract Kendig signed includes

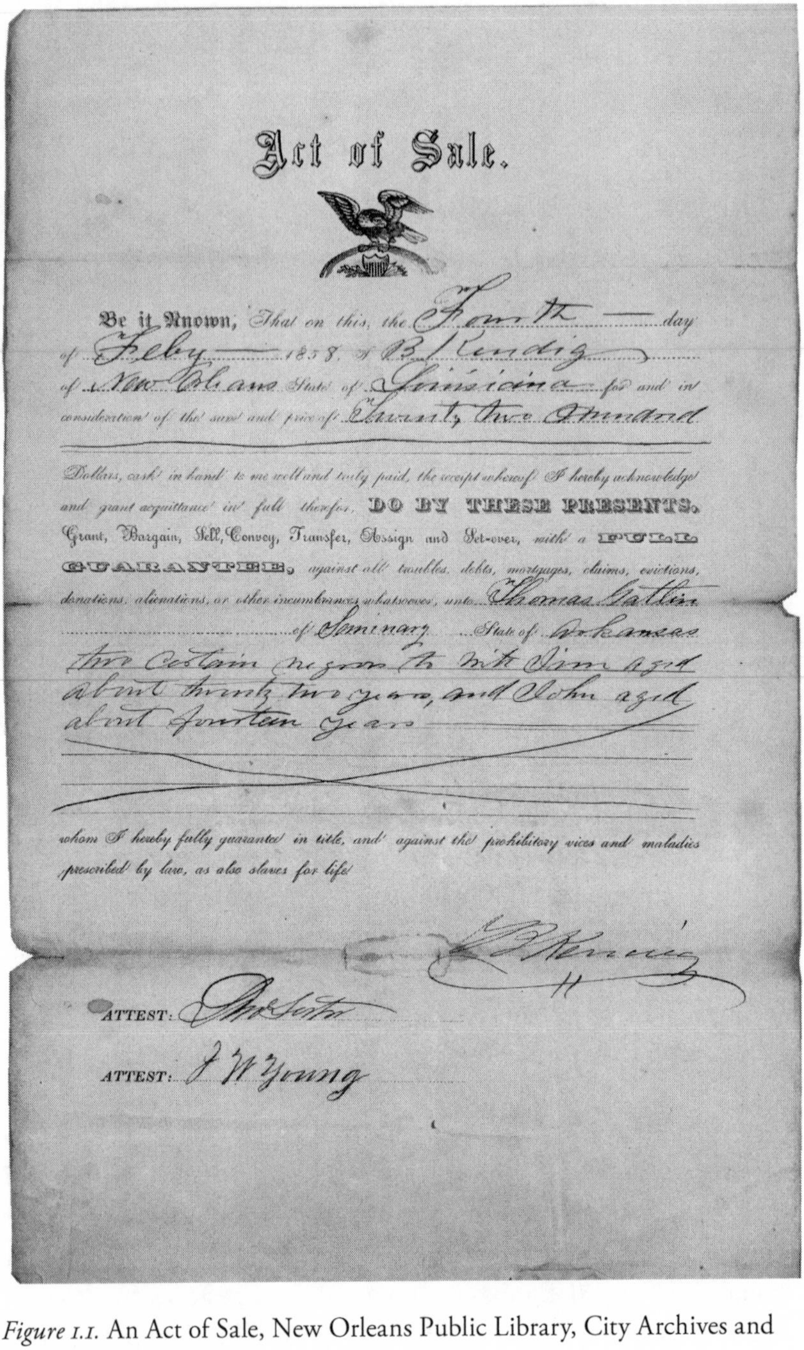

Figure 1.1. An Act of Sale, New Orleans Public Library, City Archives and Special Collections.

few details about the people he sold. The following is the extent of the biographical information about Jim Gall and John that Kendig and Gatlin included in their act of sale: "two certain negroes to wit Jim aged about twenty two years, and John aged about 14 years." These last five words, "John aged about 14 years," mark the only discernible evidence of John's life in the written record. This is, I argue, the result of antebellum enslavers' active, deliberate efforts to structure and limit what others could learn about John. Taking a closer look at how acts of sale were constructed reveals the role enslavers played in determining what and how historians can learn about the lives of enslaved people.

What we can gather about John from the written record is not there by chance. It is there because the men who enslaved John were invested in controlling what others could learn and prove about him. While this chapter is sometimes about John, it is mostly about how and why John appears and disappears in a single document. Indeed, there were at least two Johns: the first, the human being, and the second, the construct on paper. One of my goals here is to make sense of why we have access only to the second. My other goal is to do my best to learn something about John and his experiences—a task that requires doing the work necessary to make sense of how the John that survives in the written record came to be.

In exploring the production of the document that marks John's entrance and exit from the historical record, I bring to light the ways in which enslavers in antebellum New Orleans selectively documented information about the people they bought and sold. I also demonstrate that enslavers effectively, deliberately worked to define what other enslavers could learn and prove about specific enslaved individuals in the interest of incentivizing sales, securing advantageous terms, and managing risk. History has power. Enslavers knew it, and they worked to build written barriers to biographical information that the enslaved sometimes helped fortify. This chapter is an exploration of how those barriers were erected as well as an attempt to make sense of what these processes can show us about the possibilities and limits that surrounded John, as he may have understood them.

In "Venus in Two Acts," Saidiya Hartman grapples with what it means and can mean to achieve an "impossible goal": "redressing the violence that produced numbers, ciphers, and fragments of discourse, which is as close as we come to a biography of the captive and the enslaved."[2] I, too, aim to get as close as I can to a biography of John and to generate new ways we can use contracts to encounter histories of enslaved people. In my attempt to make sense of John's perspective, I imagine questions and instructions—written in italics—that represent plausible, yet unknowable conversations, instructions, and ruminations. Still, the question "Who is John?" remains impossible to answer. He is one of at least 135,000 people sold in New Orleans during the nineteenth century—one of thousands who appear and vanish in contracts, just as he did. Still, I argue, John is worthy of our study and attention.

This is not the chapter I set out to write. This chapter used to be about Jim Gall, the man sold alongside John. In Gall's case, I can trace some of his movements and actions over approximately three years, between early 1857 and May 1860. The reason for this discrepancy is fairly straightforward: Jim Gall was the subject of a lawsuit, and John was not. When Thomas Gatlin sued Bernard Kendig, he made the Fourth District Court of New Orleans into a site of historical production that centered on Gall, and none of the attorneys and witnesses who spoke during those proceedings was invested in historicizing John, save for mentioning that Gatlin also purchased him from Kendig. Our brief window into John's life slams shut soon after Bernard Kendig signed his contract, because that is what he and Thomas Gatlin wanted. All that is to say, I did not shift my focus because Jim Gall's story is not worth telling; it is. I changed course and I begin with John because what we can learn about him is more consistent with what historians of enslaved people in the nineteenth-century United States are typically able to gather about their subjects from the written record: a name, an age, a sex, and a price. And their stories are worth telling, too.[3]

Bernard Kendig, John, and Jim Gall started making decisions about what they would and would not tell a buyer before any of them set eyes on Thomas Gatlin. Kendig's calculations, however, are far easier to see than John's or Gall's. He was a local trader, well versed in the rituals of New Orleans's slave market. It is thus not out of the realm of possibility that Kendig could have told John and Jim Gall how he expected them to perform in front of potential customers. If he did, he would have considered what an enslaver would need to hear and see in order to purchase someone at a high price. And in antebellum New Orleans, securing advantageous terms involved not only working to control how enslaved people presented themselves but also using the rhetoric and culture surrounding Louisiana's redhibitory warranties to incentivize sales and transform enslaved individuals into interchangeable, valuable property on paper and over time.

Redhibitory warranties were rooted in Louisiana's redhibition laws, the state's unique brand of implied warranty regulations.[4] The state's Civil Code defined enslaved people as immovable property.[5] And those who bought and sold enslaved people in Louisiana were technically supposed to record the terms of their transactions in writing, either in an authentic act, a contract penned by a notary or public official, or under private signature, a contract penned by the parties and signed by two witnesses.[6] Additionally, sellers were "bound to two principal obligations, that of delivering and that of warranting the thing which he sells."[7] Warranting a product involved two actions on the part of a seller: first, delivering the property in question to a buyer, and second, disclosing "the hidden defects of the thing sold, or its redhibitory vices" before a sale took place.[8]

Redhibition was defined as "the avoidance of a sale on account of some vice or defect in the thing sold, which renders it either absolutely useless or its use so inconvenient and imperfect that it may be supposed that the buyer would not have purchased it, had he known the vice."[9] Louisiana's Civil Code was more specific when it came to what "hidden defects" and "redhibitory vices" were unique to enslaved people.[10] In addition to any hidden defects—behavioral or bodily traits that would not have been visible by "simple inspection" at the moment of sale—a buyer could also sue a seller for redhibition if they later discovered the person they bought was addicted to theft, had previously committed a capital crime, was in the habit of running away, or suffered from leprosy, madness, or epilepsy.[11] Dissatisfied buyers could also sue for redhibition if a seller declared that "the thing has some quality, which it is found not to have," specifically when this quality was the principal motive for making the purchase. This means that if a seller sold an enslaved person as a seamstress, for instance, and the person was subsequently found not to have said skills, the buyer could then sue for redhibition.[12]

Anyone who sold an enslaved person in Louisiana and created an act of sale could be sued for redhibition. For instance, even if the contract in which Bernard Kendig and Thomas Gatlin documented their agreement made no mention of redhibition, Gatlin could still sue Kendig for redhibition if he later discovered that John or Jim Gall suffered from a hidden or redhibitory defect that Gatlin could not have detected when he made his purchase. While sellers could modify the terms of Louisiana's implied warranty or even eliminate it entirely, they could only do so in writing and thus not without divulging information about the person they were selling. For example, a seller could warrant an enslaved person against the vices and maladies prescribed by law, save for running away and leprosy, effectively informing a buyer that an enslaved person had previously run away and suffered from leprosy. Such modifications protected sellers from future liability for the person they were selling, but because they also communicated information about an enslaved person, they could alter what a buyer was willing to pay for someone.

Enslavers cared about warranties and contracts because they were tools that helped them navigate an uncertain market, where buyer, seller, and enslaved person were all working to exert some influence over a transaction. Joseph A. Beard, a prominent New Orleans slave trader and auctioneer, believed that advertising his willingness to create an act of sale that included a full redhibitory guarantee could draw in customers, and he started mentioning them in his advertisements as early as 1840. One ad, published in New Orleans's *Daily Picayune* on May 28, 1840, announced an auction at Banks' Arcade, where Beard intended to sell 12 enslaved people between the ages of 11 and 28. Beard included additional information about some of these individuals, describing Jenny as "a good field hand" and Isaac as a "house servant and warehouseman." He also identified Robert and Dahlia as "man and wife" with an unnamed "girl child" who was between one and four months old—perhaps indicating Beard's intent to sell this particular family together. In addition to names, ages, and brief descriptions, Beard included the following at the end of his announcement: "The above sales are fully guaranteed against the vices and maladies prescribed by law, and sold for no fault. Acts of sale to be passed before J. B. Marks, notary public, at the expense of the purchasers." These last two sentences informed prospective buyers that Beard was willing to sign a notarial contract and be held liable for the people he was selling for at least a year after the sale.[13]

For enslavers, creating an act of sale was never a foregone conclusion, but sales and contracts were joined in the minds and practices of enslavers, a connection Joseph A. Beard tried to take advantage of in his advertisements. In August 1858, he published another ad, this time for an auction that would take place at noon the following day. Along with the names of 11 enslaved individuals, Beard included descriptions of their respective ages and skillsets as well as the terms under which he intended to sell them. For instance, Beard was willing to sell Frank, a 23-year-old "good engineer"; Ben, a 25-year-old "good saw miller"; and George, a 26-year-old "first-rate axeman and drayman," under several months credit "for approved endorsed notes, with a mortgage until final payment" and with a contract created before notary D. L. McKay. But Augustine, a "mulatto," "creole slave, aged 16 years, first rate house boy and coachman" and William, "aged 28 years, good axeman and sawmiller," would be sold under different terms: "one half cash, balance 6 months, for notes endorsed to the satisfaction of the vendor, with mortgage until final payment." When communicating information about the remaining six individuals he was trying to sell, Beard identified them by name, age, and skill set; he also declared that acts of sale for them would be passed before a different notary, J. B. Marks, "at the expense of the purchasers." Finally, he indicated he would sell five of the remaining six enslaved people with a full redhibitory guarantee, except for John, "a Creole boy, aged about 18 years, good carpenter, fully guaranteed, excepting once having absconded."[14]

Joseph A. Beard encouraged enslavers to attend his auctions with his descriptions of enslaved people as well as the terms and documents with

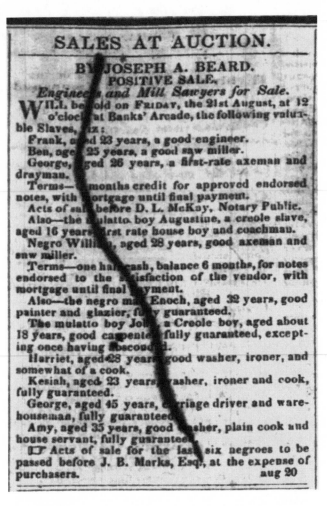

SALES AT AUCTION.

BY JOSEPH A. BEARD.
POSITIVE SALE.
Engineers and Mill Sawyers for Sale.

WILL be sold on FRIDAY, the 21st August, at 12 o'clock at Banks' Arcade, the following valuable Slaves, viz:

Frank, aged 23 years, a good engineer.

Ben, aged 25 years, a good saw miller.

George, aged 26 years, a first-rate axeman and drayman.

Terms—months credit for approved endorsed notes, with mortgage until final payment.

Acts of sale before D. L. McKay, Notary Public.

Also—the mulatto boy Augustine, a creole slave, aged 16 years, first rate house boy and coachman.

Negro William, aged 28 years, good axeman and saw miller.

Terms—one half cash, balance 6 months, for notes endorsed to the satisfaction of the vendor, with mortgage until final payment.

Also—the negro man Enoch, aged 32 years, good painter and glazier, fully guaranteed.

The mulatto boy John, a Creole boy, aged about 18 years, good carpenter, fully guaranteed, excepting once having absconded.

Harriet, aged 28 years, good washer, ironer, and somewhat of a cook.

Kesiah, aged 23 years, washer, ironer and cook, fully guaranteed.

George, aged 45 years, carriage driver and warehouseman, fully guaranteed.

Amy, aged 35 years, good washer, plain cook and house servant, fully guaranteed.

☞ Acts of sale for the last six negroes to be passed before J. B. Marks, Esq., at the expense of purchasers.   aug 20

Figure 1.2. "Sales at Auction," *Daily Picayune* (New Orleans), August 20, 1840.

which he was willing to sell each person, which included notarial contracts, extended credit and payment plans, endorsed notes, mortgage agreements, and full and mitigated redhibitory guarantees. His actions suggest that contracts as well as how they were produced and preserved mattered to enslavers. While testifying in a lawsuit tried before the Fifth District Court of New Orleans in May 1849, Beard made explicit what he suggested in his advertisements. "It frequently happens with other traders," he testified, "that purchasers require a City guarantee, and it is sometimes done as a matter of business and at others as a matter of courtesy." "It daily happens," he continued, "when the vendor is not known, that purchasers require city guarantee and particularly when the slaves come from common law states."[15]

South Carolina, North Carolina, and Louisiana were states with implied warranty regulations, meaning a buyer could sue a seller to cancel a sale regardless of whether they purchased the enslaved person in question with a warranty. In common-law states, such as Missouri, buyers were free to request warranties from sellers, but they did not enjoy the security of implied warranties. Perhaps when Joseph A. Beard compared buying enslaved people in New Orleans and in common-law states, he was referencing this particular difference. The fact that he made such a comparison suggests that enslavers, or at the very least slave traders, were well aware of the regulations pertaining to sales in different states. It also tells us that in New Orleans, enslavers valued and used the cultural meaning and legal function of redhibition laws to help them navigate sales and condense human beings into valuable commodities. It was how enslavers understood redhibitory guarantees that made them worth using and, in some cases, worth offering outside of Louisiana.[16]

On October 15, 1852, for instance, the following announcement appeared on the second page of the *Natchez (MS) Daily Courier*: "Griffin & Pullum have established themselves at the Forks of the road, Natchez, where they intend establishing a permanent Slave Depot. They have servants of all kinds for sale."[17] With that, Pierce Griffin and W. A. Pullum started selling enslaved people at Forks of the Road, a slave market just outside of Natchez, Mississippi.[18] Although Griffin and Pullum were based in Mississippi, they published advertisements that used the Louisiana guarantee to attract buyers. On November 11, 1857, in the *Mississippi Free Trader*, Griffin and Pullum announced that they had imported to the Natchez market more than 100 enslaved people from Virginia and Kentucky who were now available for purchase. "With reference to the age, soundness of body and general healthiness, as well as freedom from the vices prescribed by law," the advertisement reads, "the undersigned are prepared to give full satisfaction to their former customers."[19] In December 1858, in Natchez's *Weekly Democrat*, they offered prospective

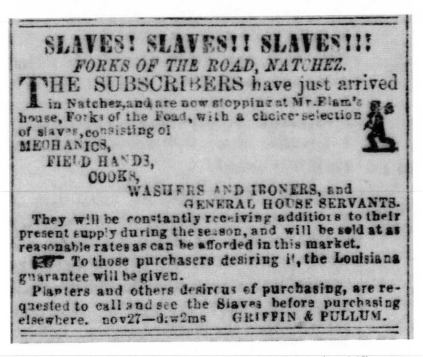

Figure 1.3. "Slaves! Slaves!! Slaves!!!," *Weekly Democrat* (Natchez, MS), December 29, 1858.

buyers the "Louisiana guarantee." "To those purchasers desiring it," the ad reads, "the Louisiana guarantee will be given." Griffin and Pullum continued including references to redhibitory vices and maladies in their advertisements until at least May 1859.[20]

Court records from redhibition suits also suggest that the significance of a redhibitory guarantee was not confined to New Orleans or to enslavers who were residents of Louisiana. The state's residents were not the only enslavers who sued one another for redhibition. Thomas Gatlin was a resident of Ouachita County, Arkansas, when he sued Bernard Kendig for redhibition in 1860. In the Orleans Parish Court—one of two civil courts that presided over disputes in New Orleans between 1813 and 1846—residents of Mississippi, Virginia, Georgia, Kentucky, Tennessee, and Alabama sued or were sued for redhibition. And when you look at the witnesses who testified in these disputes and their respective places of residence, the world these lawsuits reached out and touched expands even further. When an enslaved man by the name of Jack Smith found himself at the center of a redhibition suit tried in the Second District Court of New Orleans in 1855, enslavers and their attorneys called on witnesses from New Orleans and Baton Rouge, Louisiana; Independence, Missouri; and San Jose, California.[21] Because plaintiffs and defendants in these disputes needed to construct a well-evidenced version of the past, their scope and focus often reflected both the workings of the domestic slave trade and the coerced movements of the enslaved. What transpired during New Orleans's redhibition suits reflected the values, ambitions, and strategies of enslavers across the slaveholding United States. While not every antebellum enslaver bought or sold someone with a redhibitory warranty and even fewer sued one another for redhibition, all enslavers were invested in gathering and controlling information about the people they owned. Commodification was a process that took place on paper and over time. Because plaintiffs and defendants in redhibition suits were invested in reconstructing that process, these sources provide an invaluable glimpse of the business of slavery, the world as it then was, and how enslavers endeavored to control and exploit biographical information about the enslaved.[22]

On April 15, 1822, William Brown and Gilbert Vance, both white, male residents of New Orleans, went before notary Greenbury Ridgely Stringer to create a notarial contract. According to the authentic act of sale that Stringer created, in exchange for $950, Brown sold Vance an enslaved woman named Betsey, whom they agreed to describe as follows: "a mulatress slave named Betsey, aged about twenty two years, whom he purchased of William Bosworth by act passed before me Notary on the twenty third day of January last, and she is hereby warranted free from all debts, liens, mortgages, incumbrances as it also appears by certificate of the Recorder of Mortgages for this State dated this day; and exhibited to the parties at and before the signing hereof; warranted also free from the vices and maladies provided against by law."

There are at least three elements of this contract, which William Brown and Gilbert Vance both signed, that merit our attention. First is the fact that Brown and Vance chose to pay a notary to create an authentic act of sale, which Louisiana's Civil Code defined as "full proof of

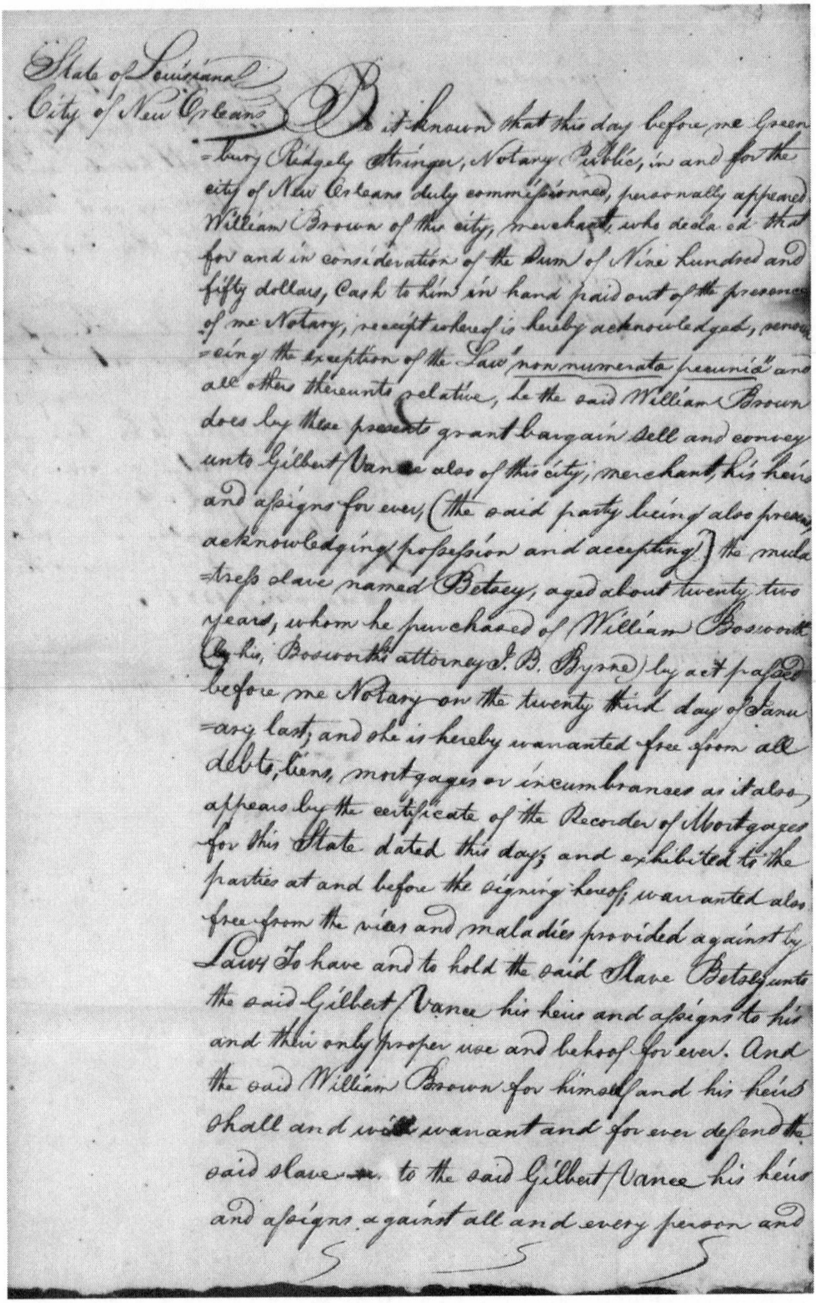

State of Louisiana
City of New Orleans

Be it known that this day before me Greenbury Ridgely Stringer, Notary Public, in and for the
city of New Orleans duly commissionned, personally appeared
William Brown of this city, merchant, who declared that
for and in consideration of the Sum of Nine hundred and
fifty dollars, Cash to him in hand paid out of the presence
of me Notary, receipt whereof is hereby acknowledged, reno-
cing the exception of the Law "non numerata pecunia" and
all others thereunto relative, he the said William Brown
does by these presents grant bargain sell and convey
unto Gilbert Vance also of this city; merchant, his heirs
and assigns for ever, (the said party being also present
acknowledging possession and accepting) the mula-
tress slave named Betsey, aged about twenty two
years, whom he purchased of William Bosworth
(by his, Bosworth's attorney J. B. Byrne) by act passed
before me Notary on the twenty third day of January last; and she is hereby warranted free from all
debts, liens, mortgages or incumbrances as it also
appears by the certificate of the Recorder of Mortgages
for this State dated this day; and exhibited to the
parties at and before the signing hereof, warranted also
free from the vices and maladies provided against by
Law. To have and to hold the said Slave Betsey unto
the said Gilbert Vance his heirs and assigns to his
and their only proper use and behoof for ever. And
the said William Brown for himself and his heirs
shall and will warrant and for ever defend the
said slave — to the said Gilbert Vance his heirs
and assigns against all and every person and

Figure 1.4. A Notarial Contract, New Orleans Public Library, City Archives
and Special Collections.

persons whomsoever by these presents. Thus done and
passed at New Orleans aforesaid this fifteenth day of
April in the year one thousand eight hundred and
twenty two, in presence of Lewis McTaney and Hugh
K. Gordon, witnesses, who hereunto sign their names
with the parties and me Notary —

(Signed) Wm Brown — Gilb. Vance — Hugh K. Gordon
— L. McTaney — & R. Stringer Not. Pub.

I certify the foregoing to be a true copy
of the Original extant in my current
Register: In faith whereof I grant these
presents under my Signature and
Seal of Office at New Orleans this
tenth day of July 1822 —

R. Stringer
Not. Pub.

the agreement contained in it." While private acts of sale, contracts signed by the parties involved alone, were legitimate contracts that created tangible obligations between parties, creating a notarial act of sale or bringing a private bill of sale to a notary or the parish recorder to document added an additional archival dimension to the process of selling a human being that was not lost on enslavers. By creating authentic acts of sale, notaries did not simply transcribe the terms of a sale; they also produced credible, valuable historical information—at least to enslavers—about the person sold. When William Brown and Gilbert Vance went before Greenbury Stringer, the notary created and archived a written, accessible record of the sale, while also conferring with the office of the recorder of mortgages to determine whether Brown had an outstanding mortgage on Betsey. By obtaining a "certificate of the Recorder of Mortgages"—a piece of paper signed and sealed by the recorder of mortgages to demonstrate whether William Brown had ever mortgaged Betsey in Orleans Parish—Stringer confirmed that Brown had not mortgaged Betsey (at least not under his own name in Orleans Parish).[23] Notaries thus performed valuable, important functions in the everyday business of slavery. They not only created contracts but also stored them and provided enslavers with access to those contracts. Effectively, notaries created, legitimized, and preserved the evidence of enslavement that enslavers used to cement their ties to one another and the people they enslaved.[24]

To turn back to the other important elements of William Brown and Gilbert Vance's contract, the second thing we should notice about this particular document is that Brown decided to divulge additional information about Betsey's past that Greenbury Stringer included in the act of sale—specifically, from whom Brown had purchased Betsey and when. This was important information that might be of use to Vance if he decided to sue Brown for redhibition, as establishing cause for redhibition often required historical information about a specific enslaved individual. And finally, Brown warranted Betsey as "free from the vices and maladies prescribed by law," meaning he made himself liable for Betsey's health, behavior, and utility for at least a year following the sale.

Enslavers, buyers and sellers alike, created contracts to communicate valuable information to other enslavers about the people they owned. They could increase their profit margin by putting a warranty—one that technically applied to any property sale documented in Louisiana—in writing, and so they often did. For William Brown and Gilbert Vance, decisions about their agreement went beyond haggling over a price. For both men, the information they documented about Betsey mattered in ways that became clear six months later, when Vance sued Brown for redhibition in Louisiana's First District Court. In his petition, Vance's attorney alleged that before the sale, Betsey, unbeknownst to Vance, was in the habit of running away, and he asked the court to cancel the transaction. In way of a response, Brown and his lawyer produced a letter addressed to Brown from Vance. The letter, dated April 15, 1822, was a significant piece of evidence that convinced the court to dismiss Vance's lawsuit rather quickly. The letter, in its entirety, reads as follows:

Mr. William Brown,
Dear sir, I acknowledge to have received from you the mulattress slave Betsey in virtue of the act of sale of this date in Mr. Stringers' office. Although full guarantee is given in this act against the vices and maladies, I acknowledge that I am acquainted with the affair in which Betsey was accused of being an accomplice or privy to a theft, for which, after absenting herself three days, and returning of her own accord, you had her imprisoned, whipped, notwithstanding that no direct proof could be brought against. Therefore, to prevent the character of the wench from being unnecessarily injured by a declaration of these circumstances in a public act, I take this mode of absolving you from all guarantee to which the Law would hold you this said act, for so much as relates to the above mentioned affair.
I am your obedient servant, Gil. Vance
New Orleans, April 15, 1822

Gilbert Vance's letter was never supposed to be made public. He and William Brown alone were to know of its existence. As to why Vance believed he could sue for redhibition when such a letter existed, I have no earthly idea. The fact that Vance wrote it at all tells us that before

Brown and Vance signed their notarial contract, Brown provided Vance with specific information about Betsey's past, information that Brown would have instructed notary Greenbury Stringer to include in the contract in the form of a mitigated redhibitory guarantee, were it not for Vance's insistence that they do otherwise. In Vance's letter, wherein he acknowledges precisely what information Brown disclosed, he divulges how he understood an act of sale: as a public record that contained information about someone he was about to own and might one day wish to sell with a full redhibitory guarantee. Vance's claim that not including said information about Betsey in the contract would protect her "character" should not be mistaken as an attempt to protect Betsey's personal reputation. On the contrary, Vance was safeguarding his own ability to define her as a valuable commodity, to sell her with a full redhibitory guarantee later, and, if necessary, to deny that he had any previous knowledge of Betsey's history of theft and running away. Had Vance and Brown instructed notary Stringer to include a mitigated warranty in their contract, they would have created a public record that established not only that Betsey was Vance's property but also that she had a past that diminished her utility and value; in that case, if Vance decided to sell Betsey with a full guarantee and Betsey absconded or stole, all an imaginary dissatisfied buyer would have to do to sue Vance and establish cause for redhibition would be to request a copy of the contract from Stringer.[25]

Contracts were never inevitable. When a buyer agreed to purchase an enslaved person, the buyer considered whether to create an act of sale and what information to include therein. In the case of William Brown, he disclosed information about Betsey that Gilbert Vance wanted. Brown also requested a letter that would privately release him from any liability involved in selling Betsey with a full redhibitory guarantee. That is not to say that when enslavers bought human beings in New Orleans, they were not seeking out accurate information about the person they were purchasing; only that there was a space between the exchange of information between buyer, seller, and enslaved person and the preservation of information about the person being sold. Enslavers knew it, and they relied on redhibition laws to make that space work to their advantage.

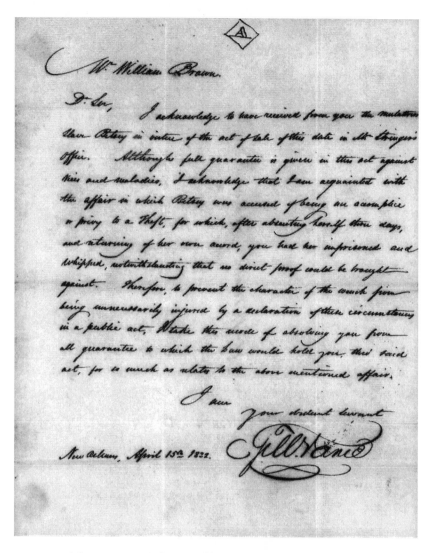

Figure 1.5. A Letter, New Orleans Public Library, City Archives and Special Collections.

In a market where another person's reputation and business practices were not always easily discernible and an enslaved person's history and future were never entirely knowable, enslavers made acts of sale and redhibitory warranties into tools of the trade. For buyers and sellers who were sometimes strangers to one another, creating contracts with guarantees was a means of reassuring themselves that even if the other party had deceived them or failed to keep up with payments over time, they still had a contract: evidence of the terms of a sale and the extended obligations of buyer and seller that Louisiana's courts could enforce.

Of course, enslavers could not do the work of constructing redhibitory guarantees alone. They needed enslaved people to perform as valuable commodities in the marketplace, in the future, and in contracts, where the enslavers flattened human beings into products to help them secure advantageous terms, manage risk, and control information over time. By the time Bernard Kendig and John met Thomas Gatlin, Kendig may have already told John what information about himself and his past to relay to prospective buyers. Sellers were always looking for the right story, one that they demanded that enslaved people corroborate with their demeanor, physical appearance, and words. Whatever John did and did not say about himself would impact Kendig's bottom line. The local trader could go on and on about John's youth, health, strength, and submissive disposition, but a buyer would most always look to John for confirmation. John knew it, and so did Kendig.

For slave traders like Bernard Kendig, preparing the people they enslaved for sale was a process, one that Solomon Northup recalled in vivid detail. For Theophilus Freeman, a New Orleans slave trader, this process began early in the morning, when he used the "sharp crack of the whip about the ears" to rouse enslaved men, women, and children from their sleep. He ordered each of them to "wash thoroughly, and those with beards to shave." He gave each of them a new suit, one Northup described as "cheap, but clean." The men wore a "hat, coat, shirt, pants, and shoes," while the women dressed in "frocks of calico, and handkerchiefs to bind about their heads." Then, they were ushered into "a large room in the front part of the building to which the yard was attached, in order to be properly trained, before the admission of customers." Freeman separated the men and women and ordered them to line up along the wall according to their respective height, from tallest to shortest. For families and friends in the room, this may have been a moment when they endured physical separation. Perhaps some tried to slouch or stand on their toes in an attempt to not only stay close to their people but also, hopefully, find a way to be sold together. After instructing them to line up, Northup wrote, "Freeman charged us to remember our places." "[Freeman] exhorted us to appear smart and lively—sometimes threatening, and again, holding out various inducements. During the day he exercised us in the art of 'looking smart,' and moving to our places with exact precision." There was a choreography to the slave market that enslavers and the enslaved knew all too well.[26]

If Bernard Kendig told John how he expected him to perform in front of potential customers, his instructions may have extended beyond the physical and stretched into John's history. When men like Thomas Gatlin considered buying someone, they worked to learn about a person's past in order to make decisions in the present. As Gatlin looked at John, he pictured the future he desired most, and he imagined how he could use John to help him get there. Gatlin looked for signs, on John's body and in his words, that told him what kind of slave John was, had been, and would be. And Kendig would have started working to define what Gatlin would and could learn, via physical inspection and invasive interrogation, long before the two men set eyes on each other:

Don't say you've run away before.[27]
Tell them you're 14.[28]
Cover up those scars.[29]

Whatever demands Kendig issued, I imagine that few, if any, would have surprised John. There was what John knew about himself, where he had been, and what he wanted, and then there was the story that Kendig wanted him to tell. These were almost certainly not one and the same, but when we look back from where and when we are now, the former is far more difficult to see than the latter.

Because information about an enslaved individual was valuable, sellers and traders sometimes worked to withhold information about the past from buyers and other enslavers, in conversation and in writing. Their actions yielded consequences beyond incentivizing a sale or raising a price; they also fundamentally shaped what we can and cannot learn about the people they bought and sold.

As a local trader in the business of buying and selling human beings, Bernard Kendig regularly and deliberately made decisions regarding what information about an enslaved person to withhold, disclose, write down, and archive. According to his testimony in an 1856 civil suit, "I generally give of my private bills of sale to the notary at the time I sell."[30] Of course, his reluctance to sign a contract when he sold John and Jim to Thomas Gatlin suggests that this was not always the case. Sometimes, Kendig believed it was in his best interest to sell a person without creating a written record of the transaction. Taking a closer look at the moments when he created acts of sale and was sued for redhibition can help us understand how and to what end he and other antebellum enslavers worked to control and exploit the historical record.

While Bernard Kendig did not leave behind any personal papers, contracts that he signed and archived with New Orleans's notaries, coupled with court records from redhibition suits he was involved in, provide a lens through which to examine his business and reach some important conclusions about how he and other enslavers used and understood contracts. Technically, enslavers were supposed to create an act of sale whenever they sold someone in Louisiana, but that does not mean they did so consistently. When Kendig sold John and Jim Gall to Thomas Gatlin, he initially refused to sign a contract, as he thought it "was too binding." But there were other moments and other sales in which, as he would later testify, Kendig would "generally give of my private bills of sale to the notary at the time I sell."[31] Exploring Kendig's actions can thus help us make sense of the circumstances when it would be in the interest of a buyer, a seller, or both to document a sale or to enter into a solely verbal agreement.

Today, New Orleans's notarial archives houses thousands of contracts that depict the sale of enslaved human beings. But even if we were to count and catalog every one of these acts of sale, we would still know only the number of sales that enslavers documented and registered with the city's notaries. We would know that x number of people, *at least*, were sold in New Orleans, but there will always be transactions, experiences, and people we will never be able to get our arms around because of the deliberate actions of men and women such as Bernard Kendig.

By the time he sold Jim Gall and John to Thomas Gatlin, Kendig had bought and sold hundreds, if not thousands, of enslaved people in New Orleans. While he did not leave behind any letters or account books, his name fills the city's conveyance and notarial records from the 1850s. According to Richard Tansey's extensive analysis of New Orleans's notarial records, Kendig sold at least 758 people using notarial contracts between 1852 and 1860. Records from lawsuits tell us that Kendig was selling people in the city in as early as 1839, if not sooner. New Orleans's conveyance indexes—which list the names of buyers and sellers who participated in transactions involving enslaved people—indicate that Kendig was party to 260 transactions involving enslaved people between April 1, 1856, and March 31, 1859, including 14 sales in 1857 and 24 sales in 1858 that were documented by New Orleans notary James Graham. However, according to Graham's records, he actually documented 125 sales involving Bernard Kendig in 1857 and 1858. I do not mean to say that the city's conveyance indexes are not important windows into the business of slavery; they are where any analysis of New Orleans's antebellum notarial records should begin, if only to get a sense of which notaries specific enslavers frequented. I do mean to argue that while we cannot know how many enslaved people were sold in New Orleans, the city's notarial records can tell us how many enslaved people were sold using notarial contracts, not the total number of people sold in the city.

Jessica Marie Johnson's concept of "null values" is especially useful when discussing the unknowable number of people who were sold in New Orleans. Johnson writes, "Impossible acts of quantification marked the lives of enslaved and free women of African descent, leaving null values, or empty spaces, in the census registers."[32] The same is true for those sold in antebellum New Orleans, where enslavers did not consistently document sales in contracts, let alone preserve them in archives. Because there are an unknowable number of sales that are lost to us, quantifying New Orleans's notarial records can only tell us *at least* how many people were sold in the city. But we must go beyond acknowledging archival silences and do the work of interrogating how and to what end these silences were produced. I argue that the brief glimpses we find of enslaved individuals in these records exist because enslavers believed they were worth creating. Understanding how Bernard Kendig used New Orleans's notaries to create and preserve acts of sale can help us make sense of the relationship between archival production and the commodification of human beings whom enslavers claimed as property.

Kendig was a contracting party in 125 transactions—119 sales, five annulled sales, and one donation—in which James Graham produced and archived notarial contracts between January 1, 1857, and December 31, 1858. Kendig acted as a buyer in 52 of these transactions and a seller in 73. And the historical and biographical information contained in these contracts varied depending on how much risk the contracting parties were willing to absorb. While each of these contracts includes the same basic information about an enslaved individual—name, age, sex, and price—some contain additional information that would purportedly allow a buyer to locate an enslaved person's previous owner. Contracts from transactions that Kendig participated in allow us to glimpse how often he divulged where and from whom he purchased the people he sold. When he purchased enslaved people, sellers disclosed information about a previous owner in 27 of 52 sales. But when Kendig sold enslaved people, he disclosed information about where and from whom he purchased the person or persons in question in 3 out of 73 transactions.[33]

For instance, when Kendig sold Sam, Ephrain, and George to Andrew M. Williams and signed a notarial contract on October 19, 1857, notary James Graham noted that in addition to guaranteeing Sam, Ephrain, and George against the vices and maladies prescribed by law, Kendig also subrogated "said purchaser to all the rights and actions of warranty to which he himself is entitled against all former owners of the said slaves." For sellers, disclosing the name of a previous owner was sometimes a means of shifting liability from oneself to the previous owner. If a year had not lapsed between the seller's purchase in Louisiana and the subsequent sale, technically the previous owner's redhibitory warranty was still in effect. For instance, *Castillanos v. Pillon* (1823), a redhibition suit tried in the Orleans Parish Court and appealed to the Louisiana Supreme Court, centered on Lewis, an enslaved man whom Stephen Pillon sold to John Castillanos in New Orleans on December 16, 1822. Pillon, the defendant, argued that he was not responsible for Lewis's habits of drinking and running away because Pillon had purchased Lewis from Henry Leslie, a resident of Portsmouth, Virginia, in New Orleans earlier on the same day, thereby making Leslie liable for Lewis's value and utility for at least a year following the date of sale. In response, Leslie argued that because he had not sold Lewis with a redhibitory guarantee, he should not be held liable for any subsequent sales. He believed that by making no mention of a redhibitory warranty in the contract he had dissolved the warranty, but that was not the case. You could extinguish Louisiana's implied warranty only in writing, and because Leslie had not done so when he sold Lewis to Pillon, Leslie had effectively sold Lewis with a full redhibitory guarantee. The Orleans Parish Court and the Louisiana Supreme Court ultimately ruled in favor of the plaintiff and against the warrantor, Leslie. According to Justice J. Porter, who penned the higher court's decision, not including a warranty in a contract was "not strong enough to release the seller from the warranty which the law raises from the sale." Leslie had sold Lewis in Louisiana, where a buyer could sue for redhibition "unless the seller had stipulated that he should be under no kind of warranty."[34]

Disclosing the name of a previous owner could thus be a way of mitigating the risks involved in selling someone in Louisiana; but divulging that information could also provide buyers with a means of securing evidence other than a contract, such as testimony, specifically in cases when they decided to sue for redhibition. By not explicitly stating, in conversation and on paper, where and from whom they had purchased the person in question, sellers, often with the help of the enslaved, erected archival walls to additional, verifiable historical information about a specific enslaved individual, walls that enslaved people such as John and Jim Gall helped fortify and that Thomas Gatlin encountered when he attempted to sue Bernard Kendig for redhibition.

I do not know what Kendig told John to say to prospective buyers, but using what I do know about Gatlin and the eventual sale, I can draw some conclusions about how Gatlin perceived John and, in turn, how John may have contributed to this perception. Gatlin went to New Orleans because he needed enslaved people to build and maintain his cotton plantation.[35] He made the journey from southern Arkansas with his friend and neighbor, James B. Milner, likely via steamboat on Bayou Bartholomew.[36] When they arrived in the city in early February 1858, Gatlin would have had plenty of people to choose from. Advertisements from the *Daily Picayune* suggest that most anywhere Gatlin and Milner walked in the French Quarter, they would have found someone for sale. If they wandered down Magazine, westward from Gravier, they may have run into Joseph A. Beard and whoever was left of the 150 enslaved people he had been trying to sell since December of the previous year.[37] If Gatlin and Milner instead headed north along Gravier, they may have encountered C. F. Hatcher, another trader, no doubt just as eager to strike a bargain.[38] But of course, not every seller or trader was in the habit of advertising so consistently. At some point during their journey, Gatlin and Milner met Bernard Kendig, who maintained a regular presence in New Orleans but whose name often went unmentioned in local newspapers.

I do not know how Kendig, Milner, and Gatlin met. I do know that whatever Gatlin learned on or by February 4 convinced him that it was in his best interest to purchase John and Jim Gall from Kendig. This process of gathering information about John and Gall was not as simple as Gatlin deciding he wanted to know something and then learning it. He had to contend with John, Gall, and Kendig, each of whom had already made important decisions about what he would and would not disclose to a buyer. There were almost certainly details about himself, his past, and his aspirations that John would never have disclosed to Kendig or Gatlin. As a person who looked to enslavers as though he was 14 years old, John was no blank slate. He had knowledge and experiences of his own, ones that taught him about loss and the terrifyingly unknowable possibilities that were always on the other side of a sale. And as free men and women ran their hands over his body, put their fingers inside his mouth, and asked him questions that sounded more like orders than requests, he may have done his best to outwardly appease Kendig while also trying to discreetly steer conversations toward the best outcome he could imagine.[39] Solomon Northup would later describe this process of enslavers examining him "precisely as a jockey examines a horse, which he is about to barter for our purchase."[40] But that is not to say that John was eager to be sold, only that in the face of miserable options, he probably tried to make the best choices he could for himself and his future. While we cannot know where those places were, there were undoubtedly places John wanted to be. It is thus not out of the realm of possibility that he covertly attempted to dissuade buyers who would take him farther from his people, while encouraging others who resided in closer proximity. Maintaining the constant vigilance necessary to navigate these interactions must have been exhausting.

As Thomas Gatlin worked to learn about John, John worked to learn about Gatlin. Solomon Northup remembered gathering just as much information about those who decided not to purchase him as those who eventually did. When an "old gentleman, who said he wanted a coachman, appeared to take a fancy" to Northup, he strained to listen to the man's conversation with Burch, Theophilus Freeman's partner. "From his conversation with Burch," Northup later wrote, "I learned he was a resident of the city. I very much desired that he would buy me, because I conceived it would not be difficult to make my escape from New-Orleans on some northern vessel."[41] John may have gathered similar information about Gatlin by conversing, observing from a distance, or both. John could have taken in Gatlin's words, clothing, smell, and demeanor, as all helped him imagine a life wherein Gatlin claimed him as enslaved property. Looking at John, Gatlin imagined his future. And when John looked back, he did, too, asking questions, dreaming up answers, and dreading the possibilities.[42]

Where would he take me?
What does he want?
What will he want?

But John would not have looked just to Thomas Gatlin for information; he would also have learned by conversing with and watching others, enslavers and enslaved individuals alike. Maybe John observed how those around him worked to navigate their circumstances, gathering valuable information by watching transactions unfold. Perhaps, like Solomon Northup, John looked on as enslavers purchased some families together while forcibly separating others.[43] Here, in the midst of misery, loss, and devastating goodbyes, John may have recalled the moments when he experienced the same. Then again, the sale to Thomas Gatlin could have severed John's proximity to one or more persons whom Bernard Kendig also claimed as his property. If it did so, we cannot know it, because for enslavers in New Orleans, only certain relationships among the enslaved were worth documenting in contracts—namely, that of mothers and their children.[44]

On June 7, 1806, the Territory of Orleans's legislature passed "an Act prescribing the rules and conduct to be observed with respect to Negroes and other Slaves of this territory," more commonly known as the Black Code, which remained in effect throughout the antebellum period. According to Section 9, "every person is expressly prohibited from selling, separately from their mothers, the children who have not attained the full age of ten years."[45] When enslavers sold children under the age of 10 years, they typically sold them with their mother and documented the relationship between mother and child. But I suspect that the law seldom stopped enslavers from selling a child under the age of 10 years alone. While the ages enslavers decided to record in contracts cannot tell us for certain how old a child was at the moment of sale, they can help us understand, first, whether enslavers consistently adhered to this particular regulation and, second, which familial relationships enslavers considered worth recording.

According to contracts that Bernard Kendig signed and James Graham notarized between January 1, 1857 and December 31, 1858, Kendig bought and sold 61 children, between the ages of eight months and 18 years, in 50 transactions. In 11 of these sales, 22 children—between the ages of eight months and 10 years of age—were sold with their respective mothers, but 9-year-old Netta was sold alone. Kendig purchased Netta on June 1, 1857, in a contract in which he and the seller described Netta as an "orphan." But when Kendig sold her just over a month later, on July 3, he and the buyer made no mention of Netta's parentage, even though they still listed her as 9 years of age. Someone in the room when Kendig purchased Netta, likely the seller, insisted that they record that Netta was an orphan as a gesture toward Louisiana's market regulations. But the fact that the end result, a sale, was the same in both cases tells us that while enslavers sometimes sold enslaved children with their mothers and believed those relationships were worth recording—indeed, they were the only relationships that enslavers believed were worth recording—they did not do so consistently.

Even if John had siblings, parents, or friends in Bernard Kendig's yard in February 1858, Kendig would have had no reason to document those relationships in a contract. What he did write down tells us at least two things: first, that making children into orphans was always part of his despicable business and, second, that the law did not and could not have stopped him from destroying families to line his pockets. With deliberate efforts to define John as a valuable commodity, Kendig rendered John's relationships, whom he cared about and where they were, permanently hidden from our view.

Three months after Thomas Gatlin bought John and Jim Gall from Kendig, Gall escaped; unable to locate Gall, Gatlin left his Arkansas plantation and returned to New Orleans to ask Kendig for a refund. After listening to Gatlin's request, Kendig refused, and Gatlin decided to sue Kendig for redhibition. He went to consult Louis E. Simonds and Charles E. Fenner, partners in a New Orleans law firm. They listened to Gatlin's story and responded with a phrase that was perhaps not so far removed from what ran through Kendig's mind when Gatlin approached him earlier that day: that to sue for redhibition and win, Gatlin would need to "prove the existence of the vice of running away, previous to the sale." He could not simply assert that Gall had absconded since Gatlin purchased him but also had to demonstrate that Gall was in the habit of running away before the sale, and that information was not necessarily easy to come by, at least not for Gatlin. He had a contract that led him to Bernard Kendig and to Jim Gall but nowhere else. Gall was gone, and Kendig—who had been sued for redhibition at least nine times before Gatlin purchased Gall—was certainly not going to divulge any information that would help Gatlin build a case. He thus had neither the knowledge nor the evidence necessary to sue Kendig for redhibition and win. This was not by chance. It was the result of deliberate decisions that Kendig made at the level of the sale, a contract, and the archive.[46]

Bernard Kendig knew how to manipulate the written record. He signed contracts with redhibitory warranties to help incentivize sales and secure advantageous terms, and he was careful about what he revealed in the process. Using New Orleans's notaries, Kendig thus worked to exert some control over what a buyer could learn and prove about the people they purchased. I do not mean to suggest that every person who sold another in New Orleans knew how to create and exploit archival silences; they almost certainly did not. I do mean to argue that producing historical and archival silences, limiting what other enslavers could learn about a specific enslaved individual such as John, was always part of buying and selling enslaved human beings in New Orleans. The document that allows us to encounter John as a name, an age, a sex, and a price alone is an enduring testament to the effectiveness of his methods. Court records from *Gatlin v. Kendig* (1859) provide further insight into the information that Kendig used contracts to not reveal.

Unbeknownst to Thomas Gatlin when he purchased John and Jim Gall from Bernard Kendig, he was not the first person to buy Gall from Kendig. A year earlier, Kendig sold Gall to a Texas lawyer by the name of John F. Williams for either $1,300 or $1,400. Soon afterward, Williams transported Gall to his home in Marshall, Texas, located just west of Shreveport, Louisiana. Gall remained in Texas for at most a year, and during that time—at least according to John F. Williams—Gall absconded twice. The first time, three months after arriving in Marshall, Gall was captured and imprisoned as a runaway in the Rusk County jail, located in Henderson, Texas, some 40 miles from Williams's farm. When Williams learned where Gall was, he went to Henderson to claim him and brought him back to Marshall, and a week later, Jim Gall escaped again. This time, he traveled 400 miles southwest to Gillespie County, Texas, where he was captured and imprisoned as a runaway in Fredericksburg. After retrieving Gall from another Texas jail, Williams decided to bring Gall back to New Orleans and to ask Bernard Kendig to honor the terms of his warranty and cancel the sale.[47]

When buyers returned to ask sellers to honor the terms of a redhibitory warranty, sellers used their discretion as well as what they knew about the market and the law to determine whether it was in their best interest to cancel a sale. Bernard Kendig decided to comply with John F. Williams's request and accept Jim Gall because—after interrogating and examining Gall—Kendig arrived at the conclusion that he could once more sell him at a profit, at least in part because Gall looked like a slave who was free from the vices and maladies prescribed by law. But there were also moments when Kendig refused to cancel sales. On August 9, 1854, in New Orleans, he sold an enslaved man named Dick to James Riggin, also a resident of New Orleans. Eleven months later, at least according to Riggin, Dick escaped and hid in the woods not far from his home. By the time Riggin captured him, Dick was "in a dying condition from the disease contracted by him during his absence as a runaway and being the immediate consequence of his exposure." Afterward, in July 1855, Riggin brought Dick back to New Orleans to ask Bernard to cancel the sale, take Dick back, and issue a refund. After listening to Riggin's request, Kendig examined and interrogated Dick, and calculated what another enslaver might be willing to pay for him and whether James Riggin had sufficient evidence to establish cause for redhibition in court. After doing the math, Kendig decided it was not in his interest to cancel the sale, explaining, "he would not take back a sick or dead negro."[48] In way of a response, Riggin asserted that "he could prove that the boy was a runaway" and threatened Kendig with a redhibition suit, to which Kendig replied, "I will defend it."[49]

When John F. Williams brought Jim Gall back to New Orleans, in either late January or early February 1858, Bernard Kendig came to a different decision. He thought about what he knew about the law and the market, he made his calculations, and he decided that he and Gall could convince a buyer that Gall was a sound slave and a sound investment. As long as he could still sell Gall with a full redhibitory guarantee, there was still space to turn a profit. But Kendig's calculations—his active, deliberate decisions regarding what information about the enslaved to disclose, withhold, and document—could yield important consequences beyond the contents of a contract. They could also affect the lives of enslaved people, because men like Bernard Kendig needed the human beings they sold to perform their commodification, to behave, speak, and move according to standards, ideals, and ambitions that enslavers refined using redhibitory guarantees, at the moment of sale and in the future.

Bernard Kendig could not sell John and Jim Gall to Thomas Gatlin with a full redhibitory guarantee without John and Gall's respective cooperation, which Kendig may have ensured through negotiations, coercion, threats, or violence. But that is not to say that John and Gall did not have their own reasons for performing as enslaved individuals free from the vices and maladies prescribed by law. In Gall's case, it was in his interest for Gatlin not to know that he had escaped at least three times in the previous year, twice from John F. Williams's East Texas farm and once from Bernard Kendig's yard, not long after Williams returned Gall. That bit of information might disincentivize Gatlin's purchase, but if he followed through with the sale, it might also have influenced how he treated, surveilled, and endeavored to control Jim Gall on the road to Arkansas and in the future.

John Brown, a free man of color who was enslaved and eventually escaped to London, England, where he penned a narrative detailing his experiences in Georgia, recalled the immediate effects of being sold with a full redhibitory guarantee. While he was imprisoned in Theophilus Freeman's pen in New Orleans, Louisiana—likely during the 1840s—Brown learned that to be "sold as a 'guaranteed nigger'" was to be "warranted not to run away. In such cases," Brown continued, "should the man bolt, the seller is obliged to refund the sum he received for him." Later, a man by the name of Jepsey James purchased John Brown and several other enslaved people from Theophilus Freeman. And while the others who James purchased "were at once chained and handcuffed," Brown wrote, "Freeman guaranteed me, so I was not served so."[50]

I have no illusions that the time when Jepsey James claimed John Brown as his property involved excessive freedom of mobility. The day after arriving on James's cotton plantation, Brown and the other enslaved people on the property were awakened at 4 a.m. and forced to pick cotton until nightfall. If Brown noticed any further connections between how James treated him and the terms of the sale in New Orleans, he did not make them explicit in his narrative. I do, however, think we can draw at least two conclusions from John Brown's experiences: first, that enslavers thought about redhibitory warranties when they made decisions that shaped enslaved people's lives, even after a sale took place; and, second, that enslaved people had and shared knowledge with one another regarding what specific terms of sales meant and, in turn, used this knowledge to influence and interpret the circumstances of their enslavement. John Brown used what he knew about the terms of his sale to understand his circumstances. And Jim Gall and John might have made similar calculations when Bernard Kendig sold them to Thomas Gatlin. There was information about themselves, their pasts, and what they wanted for their respective future that they deliberately withheld from both Kendig and Gatlin. They had cards to play, too, and sometimes it was worth keeping them close to the vest.

The world in which we find and lose John was one where those in power valued and worked to exploit information about him. It was their violent extractions that gave shape to John's life as well as helped to define its possibilities and limits. The moments when enslavers needed paper to facilitate the commodification of the people they claimed as property generated the evidence that we depend on to historicize those at the center of their constructions. And we remain bound by decisions that enslavers and colonizers made more than a century ago.

I lose John on the road to Thomas Gatlin's southwest Arkansas cotton plantation, some time after Gatlin purchased him from Bernard Kendig. Before the journey began, John and Jim Gall would have gathered information from Kendig and other enslaved people who were waiting to be sold alongside them, and they would have continued gathering information about Gatlin, where they were going, and what awaited them when they got there well after Kendig signed the contract. Even if John did know where they were going, I suspect he would have worked to orient himself geographically throughout the journey, not just in terms of which way was north or where the closest town was but also in terms of how much closer to or farther from his people he might be. I do not know where John's loved ones were, but he did. At the very least, he knew where they were the last time he saw them. His circumstances had changed, and it was possible that theirs had, too. Of course, John and Jim Gall may have found opportunities to converse throughout the journey as well. Perhaps Gall shared with John some of the knowledge he accumulated while in Texas. Maybe they found comfort and solidarity in each other's presence. We have no way of knowing, however, if that was the case. The question "Who is John?" is impossible to answer.[51]

For antebellum enslavers, a sale was a process of extraction and production. Enslavers gathered and invented information about specific human beings, which they then used to create valuable historical documentation in the interest of condensing people into interchangeable property on paper and in archives; but they could not always do this work without the help of enslaved individuals. When we work backward from the text of a contract to explore John's role in its making, we do the work necessary to get beyond the name, age, sex, and price that define his entrance and exit from the historical record, not as a means of simply acknowledging what we cannot learn about him but in order to make sense of the possibilities and limits that surrounded him and other enslaved people in New Orleans's marketplace and elsewhere. Buyers and sellers alike looked to John to perform his commodification, to live up to their violent cultural expectations of soundness and value, expectations they used Louisiana's peculiar market regulations to help them articulate and achieve. Thus, the circumstances of John's enslavement were such that he was most always a valuable source of information about himself—certainly not always credible or powerful, but always important. He was also a child with choices, hopes, and fears. And sometimes, he tried to shape his life and his future in what can only be described as miserable, dangerous circumstances. While I cannot know where his life took him beyond Arkansas, I can hope that wherever it was, it was somewhere John wanted to go.

CHAPTER 2

Isaac Wright

Enslavement and Historical Narratives

It was all he had. His story. A man's story is his gris-gris,
you know. Taking his story is like taking his gris-gris. The
thing that is himself.

—ISHMAEL REED, *Flight to Canada*

ON SEPTEMBER 26, 1839, in New York City, Isaac Wright was deposed in
Lawrence, Curator of McMahon v. Botts (1841), a civil suit then taking
place in New Orleans's Orleans Parish Court. Wright was 21 at the time,
and he had just returned from hell. Almost two years earlier, while working aboard the steamboat *New Castle*, Wright was lured to a New
Orleans jail, kidnapped, and enslaved. He was not alone. Stephen
Dickenson Jr. and Robert Garrison, two free men of color who worked
alongside Wright, were also enslaved.[1]

In chapter 1, I grappled with the possibilities and limits of a history
of John, an enslaved person whom we can recognize only as entering and
exiting the historical record in a single contract. How we encounter Isaac
Wright in the written record is markedly different. When it comes to
writing his history, I have access to court records; a narrative penned by
Stephen Dickenson Jr., who was enslaved alongside Wright; and Wright's
own testimony. These records include extensive evidence of Wright's experiences, as he and others recounted them. Together, these documents
allow us a glimpse of not only what were likely the most miserable times
of Wright's life but also the historical and intellectual labor that enslavers demanded of the enslaved—work that, while often undocumented,

nevertheless facilitated the commodification of enslaved people as well as shaping the circumstances of their enslavement.[2]

This chapter is about Isaac Wright, the process of his enslavement, and his quest for freedom. It is also about the coercive, violent practices that enslavers used to force those they enslaved to construct the past. It is a part of the story of enslavement that we can never know, at least not at the individual level, about people like John, who materialize and vanish in contracts. That does not make it any less real or important to our understanding of how enslaved people were forced to perform their commodification. In this chapter, I trace the moments when Isaac Wright was forced to tell false stories about the past. In doing so, I do not mean to argue that his experiences—what we can see of them from when and where we are now—were universal. Not every enslaved person was previously free; not every enslaved person experienced the horrors of the New Orleans slave market; and not all enslaved people had the opportunity to document their story themselves. I do, however, believe that there are elements of what Wright and his companions endured that tell us something essential about the kind of labor involved in enslavement: specifically, that of constructing the past to benefit someone else's future. In Isaac Wright's story, we thus have an opportunity to learn something about John's life as well as the lives of other enslaved people—not his internal life or his precise lived experiences, but certainly the expectations, demands, and violence that shaped his life and constrained his choices.

The men who kidnapped Isaac Wright, Stephen Dickenson Jr., and Robert Garrison worked hard to make their peers believe that their victims were slaves. Taking a closer look at the kidnappers' strategies for doing so demonstrates that putting recognizably Black individuals in chains was not all it took to enslave Wright, Dickenson, and Garrison. To be sure, being marked as Black mattered, and it made them vulnerable. But when we look closely at how enslavers worked to make Isaac Wright into someone who could be appraised and sold, we also see moments, over and over again, when his ability to reconstruct the past was central and essential to his commodification. Acknowledging that he was recognizably Black can help us make sense of why Wright and his companions were kidnapped, but understanding *how* they were enslaved requires that we go a step further, looking beyond the act of kidnapping and toward the process of enslaving. Indeed, because there were instances when an enslaved person's history was deemed by enslavers to be worth recounting, there were also instances when enslaved people were forced to become historians of commodities, not simply to facilitate their own exploitation but also to survive. The twists and turns required to make buyers believe they could know a human being's past and accurately predict their future depended on the intellectual and historical labor of enslaved people, work we cannot always see clearly when we read contracts alone.[3]

In Isaac Wright's experiences, we also find the terrible power that a contract could wield. With enslavers' ability to use acts of sale to construct and control histories of enslaved individuals also came the ability to erase the histories of free individuals and help transform them into slaves. While this chapter is primarily about the historical and intellectual labor that enslaved people were expected to perform, it is important that we not lose sight of the tools and processes that a free individual's history, however rooted in reality, were up against. If Isaac Wright, Stephen Dickenson Jr., and Robert Garrison's kidnappers had had their way, we would never have known that the three men they kidnapped and sold were free. And if the only written evidence we had of the three men's existence was the notarial contract that their enslavers signed on February 14, 1838, the kidnappers probably would have gotten what they wanted.

Another important part of Isaac Wright's story is how he worked to survive and escape enslavement. In his efforts to survive and secure his freedom, we see that his ability to reconstruct the past was also essential. Indeed, there were moments, carefully chosen ones, when Wright told his actual story, the one he knew to be true. These moments tell us that just as invented stories about the past could be a site of Wright's commodification, the past could also be a resource for his survival and self-expression as well as a source of his liberation. In the tension between the history enslavers needed Isaac Wright to repeat and the one he knew to be true, we find evidence that enslaved people's ability to construct the past mattered not only to enslavers but also to the enslaved. Indeed, enslaved people were historians of themselves, gathering, preserving, and sharing information about themselves that was important to them and their community. Enslavers' power over the past, while terrible, was never absolute, which means that an enslaved person's past was most always contested. In working to historicize enslaved individuals, we must thus acknowledge their active, important role in the making of their history.[4]

I found Isaac Wright by chance. As I pored over civil court records, looking for enslaved people, the petition in *Lawrence, Curator of McMahon v. Botts* (1841) caught my eye. I was used to seeing dissatisfied buyers sue sellers over illnesses and past behavior, not freedom. And in direct contrast to freedom suits, here was an enslaver working hard to demonstrate that he had purchased a free man. As I read the almost 300-page case file, I was struck by not only the horrors of Isaac Wright's experiences but also what I have come to understand as the recurring role of stories about the past in his enslavement. While his experience cannot tell us everything we might want to know about someone like John, they can help us grasp the realities that contracts were made to conceal: first, that controlling enslaved people's history was most always important to those who enslaved them; second, that enslavers' efforts to historicize the people they enslaved shaped the lives of enslaved people; and finally, that enslaved people played active, important roles in the construction of their past.

In November 1837, Captain Jonathan Dayton Wilson hired Isaac Wright, Stephen Dickenson Jr., and Robert Garrison, all free men of color, to work as firemen on board the steamboat *New Castle*. According to historian Robert H. Gudmestad, firemen "had the most physically demanding job on the steamboat." They stood over open furnaces, stacking wood and flinging it into a scalding fire in order to propel the boat forward. "The intense heat and constant motion was so arduous that they worked four-hour shifts and usually refused to work for more than two successive voyages."[5] I do not know whether Dickenson or Garrison had previously worked on a steamboat, but Wright's testimony tells us that this was his first time. Before they set sail from New York

City, he had probably worked on his grandparents' farm in Virginia, at least until he was 10 years old. His grandparents were free people, as were his parents, Fanny and Samuel Wright. After Samuel passed away, Isaac Wright and his mother moved to Philadelphia, where she believed she could "do better" than in Virginia. There, Wright served as an apprentice waiter to a man named Samuel Schrack for five years before moving to New York City, where he worked as a porter in various stores. Somehow, while in the city, Wright became acquainted with Captain Jonathan Dayton Wilson, who offered him a job that paid $20 a month.[6]

I wonder what convinced Isaac Wright to work for Captain Wilson. Perhaps it was the wages? Maybe Wright believed that working as a fireman could open more, better opportunities onboard steamboats? Could he have wanted to see another part of the country? Whatever his reasons, Wright felt safe enough about the job, one that would take him to the slaveholding United States, that he decided not to bring his freedom papers with him. In a letter he would later send to a friend in Philadelphia, Wright explained that he shipped out of New York "without free papers" but provided no explanation for why he made this particular decision. Could Wright's papers have saved him from what came next? We cannot know for certain, but I doubt it. As John Bardes's work has convincingly demonstrated, possession of freedom papers in New Orleans did not always matter, as the city's police, judges, and jailors regularly, "systematically destroyed, seized and voided" legal documentation of freedom. For people of color, especially those separated from communities that could support their claims to freedom, New Orleans could be a dangerous place.[7]

After leaving New York in November 1837, Isaac Wright, Stephen Dickenson Jr., and Robert Garrison traveled between New York, Mobile, Pensacola, St. Marks, and New Orleans. In February 1838, while docked in New Orleans, Captain Wilson told the crew he was sick and went ashore for several days, leaving Thomas Lewis in charge of the boat. During that time, Wright would later testify, Lewis moved frequently between the steamboat and the shore. Eventually, Lewis instructed Wright, Dickenson, and Garrison to accompany him into town to retrieve some hemp they would use to clean the boat's machinery. The errand was a ruse. Instead of leading them to retrieve hemp, Lewis walked Wright, Dickenson, and Garrison to New Orleans's Second Municipality jail, where he imprisoned them as the slaves of slave trader George Ann Botts.[8]

On February 14, 1838, George Ann Botts and Thomas Lewis appeared before New Orleans notary William Young Lewis. At Botts and Thomas Lewis's direction, the notary created a contract. According to the two-page document, Thomas Lewis sold Botts three enslaved men named Isaac, Stephen, and Robert, for $1,825 cash. They recorded the men's first names and ages in the contract, but they included no additional biographical information. Of course, the contract itself may have been a farce, created to demonstrate that Wright, Dickenson, and Garrison were Botts's property, not because an actual sale had taken place. Perhaps Botts, Lewis, and Captain Wilson had all conspired to share the profits of whatever sale came next. Regardless of their arrangement, Botts knew he needed a contract to make what was about to happen appear legitimate. Enslavement was a process that required not only brute force but also paper and, sometimes, archives to propel it forward.

Isaac Wright, Stephen Dickenson Jr., and Robert Garrison desperately tried telling the men who imprisoned them that they were free. At first, they refused to "acknowledge Mr. [George Ann] Botts to be their Master." They were beaten for their obstinance. Their hands and feet were tied to a ladder, Wright would later recall, and they were whipped until "they were nearly senseless." Afterward, Botts took them from the jail to his slave yard, a space filled with some fifty enslaved people, strangers who Wright thought looked like they "had been whipped and otherwise bruised to such a degree they could but just walk." There was evidence of Botts's brutality everywhere they looked, evidence that Botts used to threaten Wright, Dickenson, and Garrison into submission. In these circumstances, Botts issued a host of directions, demands, and threats of further violence.

If you think you can endure what you see, you might go free.
Never mention freedom, New York, Captain Wilson, the New Castle, *or your own names.*

If anyone asks you who you belong to, say, "Mr. Botts."
If you don't, I will kill you.[9]

Wright, Dickenson, and Garrison neither argued nor resisted. They knew that their survival depended on not only their silence but also their active participation. This means that in addition to taking in Botts's threats, they also absorbed a specific story about the past, one they memorized and readied themselves to tell. Wright's and Dickenson's testimony tell us that they believed and feared Botts. And they demonstrated their faith and terror each time they lied about who they were and where they had been—lies they would continue to tell even outside of Botts's presence. Richard Percival, who would later purchase Dickenson, remembered this story well. After he discovered Dickenson was free, he recalled asking him "how it was that he had frequently told the [Percival] family, that he had been raised in Virginia as a slave by the Botts family, kept in the house as a nurse, and that his young master had taught him to read and in consequence of the embarrassment of his Old Master, himself and two other boys were taken off and sold?" To this, Dickenson replied, "he had been forced to tell the tale to keep from being whipped."[10]

For George Ann Botts, transforming Isaac Wright, Stephen Dickenson Jr., and Robert Garrison into slaves involved a contract, imprisonment, and violence; it also required working to control how and what others, especially potential buyers, could learn about each of the three men and their respective pasts. Botts told Wright, Dickenson, and Garrison when to remain silent, when to speak, and most important, what to reveal and what to withhold. Botts fashioned a historical narrative, one that Wright, Dickenson, and Garrison committed to memory, that was not a complete fabrication. Their names, at least their first names, remained the same, but they were told to never utter their surnames again. Most everything else they learned to repeat and probably tried to make sound convincing was a lie. They described a past that never took place, one that justified their enslavement, made them seem worth purchasing, and accounted for their ability to read. It was a history that Botts thought his contemporaries would, if not wholeheartedly believe, at least consider plausible enough. Everyone lied in the slave market, and they worked to make their lies sound believable. Botts's demands tell us, first, that dishonesty mattered; second, that enslavers, even in their deceit, were most always contending with an enslaved person's past; and finally, that enslavers could seldom make their deceptions ring true without the active support of the people they enslaved.[11]

Isaac Wright would later testify that for the next three days, he, Stephen Dickenson Jr., and Robert Garrison "were examined by many individuals who came to purchase slaves," strangers who made demands of their bodies and minds. I imagine they were terrified, angry, and exhausted, not to mention physically injured. They paid attention to their surroundings. They knew they were being watched. They lied to keep from being whipped. Perhaps, as they told stories that George Ann Botts invented and that they knew to be false, they began to lose hope that they would ever escape.

My name is Isaac.   *My name is Stephen.*   *My name is Robert.*
    I belonged to the Botts family.
    I learned to read, so I was sold.[12]

While there was much about their present circumstances that remained uncertain and unknowable, Isaac Wright did know that Botts "hoped" to sell them "at private sale." While Wright might not have realized it at the time, Botts's ambition suggests that he, a professional slave trader, knew how to make paper work to his advantage. He used the local jail and a notarial contract to create written evidence of his claim to Wright, Stephen Dickenson Jr., and Robert Garrison. Then, he intended to use a private bill of sale to make them disappear. Botts's need to control the past and what others could learn about it would not end with a sale. He needed Wright, Dickenson, and Garrison to keep telling the same story; and he needed to limit what others, especially those interested in restoring their freedom, could discover about their fate. It was a means of both protecting himself from future liability and making sure the men he kidnapped remained enslaved.

After failing to sell them in New Orleans, Botts put Wright, Dickenson, Garrison, and at least two other enslaved individuals, Sam and

Aaron, onboard the steamboat *Bunker Hill*, bound for Vicksburg, Mississippi. According to Dickenson's narrative, one of these strangers, either Sam or Aaron, said he was also free.[13] Once they arrived in Vicksburg, Botts's agent, an auctioneer named John Rudisill, began trying to sell each of them.[14] He forced them to walk the streets, carrying a red flag and ringing a bell to advertise themselves for sale. Within a week, Rudisill put Wright, Dickenson, and Garrison up for auction, but as he could not secure a high enough price, Rudisill decided to hold off on selling them just yet. Eventually, Dickenson would later write, a buyer paid for them, "but in consequence of information which he drew from us, by asking questions, he began to suspect they we were free, gave up his bargain and his money was returned to him." The next day, the unnamed buyer returned to speak to Wright, Dickenson, and Garrison, just outside of Rudisill's presence. He asked them if they were free, but "having suffered already so much for saying we were free," Dickenson later recalled, "we hesitated to answer him." One of the enslaved people who had journeyed with Wright, Dickenson, and Garrison from New Orleans responded instead, explaining that he was free and had come from New York. "He then questioned us very closely, took down our narrative, and said if he had time he would write to our friends, and left us." The man then called on Rudisill, informing him that he believed Wright, Dickenson, and Garrison were free. In way of a response, Rudisill wrote to George Ann Botts and told him what was happening. Botts responded, directing Rudisill "to get rid of us," Dickenson later wrote, as soon as possible. Rudisill sold each of them soon afterward.

Make no mistake: Isaac Wright, Stephen Dickenson Jr., and Robert Garrison were forced to tell a specific story about their respective pasts. They committed it to memory. They recited it on demand. And there was violence in the repeating. We should not, however, lose sight of the fact that they were simultaneously telling other stories, too, ones they knew to be true. The fact that a person enslaved alongside them spoke up and declared that he was free and had come from New York tells us that for enslaved people, reconstructing the past was not reserved for the marketplace or the urging of a buyer and a seller. There were other moments, stolen ones, when enslaved people decided they trusted one another enough to tell the truth about who they were and where they had been. Somewhere, sometime, and at great risk to themselves, Isaac Wright, Stephen Dickenson Jr., and Robert Garrison believed they could trust at least one person who was enslaved alongside them. And this trust was as essential to their survival as the deception they were forced to perform.[15]

It is possible that John Rudisill used threats and violence to compel Wright, Dickenson, and Garrison to stop telling potential buyers that they were free men. If he did, Wright and Dickenson did not say so, at least not in the records we have access to. Whatever Rudisill's reaction to their revelation, it obviously achieved its desired end. Wright, Dickenson, and Garrison did stop telling potential buyers that they were free, at least for now. They probably also went back to reciting the historical narrative that George Ann Botts fashioned in New Orleans, one that included no mention of their surnames, freedom, or New York.

My name is Isaac.   My name is Stephen.   My name is Robert.
I belonged to the Botts family.
I learned to read, so I was sold.[16]

Isaac Wright, Stephen Dickenson Jr., and Robert Garrison's respective stories were convincing enough to secure two buyers. John McMahon, who lived about half a mile outside of Vicksburg, purchased Wright from John Rudisill on March 3, 1838. Later, he would also purchase Garrison. And James Percival bought Stephen Dickenson Jr. for his son Richard, who lived in Kentucky. "The separation was painful," Dickenson later wrote. "We had been acquainted before we left home; we had been companions on board the steam-boat New Castle several months; we had been companions in suffering in the jail at New Orleans, and from there to Vicksburgh; but now we were to be separated, I supposed, forever."[17]

After a month of working for John McMahon, and weeks of trying to slip away unnoticed, Isaac Wright finally managed to get to Vicksburg, intent on buying some paper and ink. George Ann Botts had used paper to help him make Wright into a slave, and paper, Wright hoped, just might help save him. Whoever was working at the store thwarted Wright's plan, refusing to sell him the items. Instead, they sent someone along with Wright to inform McMahon about what the man Mc-Mahon claimed as his enslaved property had attempted to purchase.

What were you going to do with paper and ink?
I was going to write a letter to my friends and mother in Philadelphia.
Are you free?
I am.
Why didn't you tell me sooner?
You didn't ask, and I thought I had no right to say anything unless
I was asked.[18]

By this point, for Isaac Wright, silence was a means of surviving. He had told the truth about who he was and where he came from, but he was not out of the woods yet. It was up to McMahon to decide what to do with his newly discovered information. Two months later, McMahon told Wright he believed he was free but did not think the same of Robert Garrison. Then, he made a proposition. Isaac would later testify:

He [John McMahon] said that I Robert [Garrison] and a female slave
named Harriet were all the property he owned, and he could not
afford to lose us, and that he would have to sell us and then he would
take the money could go down and see [John] Rudisill and try to get
his money back, and if he could not get his money from Rudisill he
would go on to Philadelphia and get Mr. [James] Hill to come on and
identify me if I would agree to serve him three years for his trouble.[19]

John McMahon aimed to double his investment in Isaac Wright, with money from a new, unsuspecting buyer and a reimbursement from John Rudisill. Wright, perhaps unable to see another way out of his present circumstances, agreed to McMahon's terms, so long as he would immediately contact James Hill. On May 2, 1838, McMahon penned a letter to Hill, asking him to send along "any paper or proof" of Wright's freedom. McMahon then took Wright to Memphis, Tennessee, where he sold him to Hinson Gift for $1,000. McMahon also sold Robert Garrison to a man by the name of William Jeter, a resident of Arkansas.

Soon after returning to his home, McMahon passed away. In the last month of his life, he coerced Isaac Wright into, once more, performing his commodification. McMahon possessed written evidence of his claim to Wright, evidence that technically would allow him to sell Wright; but he could not hope to do so if Wright refused to play his part. Again, Wright was forced to tell stories about the past that he and McMahon knew to be false. Perhaps he repeated the same story that George Ann Botts had tortured him, Stephen Dickenson Jr., and Robert Garrison into memorizing in New Orleans. Maybe McMahon came up with a new tale, one he believed would make Wright desirable and fetch a high price. Whatever shape the road to Hinson Gift's purchase took, it was one that McMahon could not have paved alone.

Wright worked for Gift, who lived not far from Raleigh, Tennessee, just outside of Memphis, for five months before finally telling his new owner that he was a free man. Gift responded by calling John McMahon a "rascal," exclaiming that those who had enslaved Wright "ought to be punished." He then promised to write to James Hill in Philadelphia, to obtain Wright's freedom papers. On August 8, 1838, Gift did, indeed, send a letter to Hill, requesting evidence of Isaac's freedom. But before Hill could respond, Gift gambled Wright away to a man named John T. Simpson, who was also a resident of Tennessee.[20]

After losing Wright to Simpson, Gift took Wright aside and told him "to say nothing" about his freedom because Simpson "would not like to have a free man in his employ." Again, Wright was asked to lie about himself and the past to benefit an enslaver. Gift could gamble Wright away without his presence, knowledge, or consent, but Gift could not hope to use Wright to cover his gambling debts if he refused to keep quiet. This time, Wright did not wait five months before telling his new owner that he was a free man. He would later testify that Simpson "allowed that all hands concerned were rascals" and told him he should go free if he was indeed a free man. Then, Simpson went off to Vicksburg, Mississippi, to see the horse races, leaving Wright at his home in Tennessee, alone.

While John Simpson was in Mississippi, Joshua Coffin—an antislavery activist from Philadelphia, whom James Hill had told about Isaac Wright's present circumstances—arrived with documentary evidence of Wright's freedom. Instead of waiting for Simpson to return, Wright decided to leave with Coffin. They walked northward to and through Illinois and Indiana, where they stayed until the river was high enough to allow for steamboat travel to Louisville, Cincinnati, and, finally, Philadelphia.

We can only imagine the fear and despair Isaac Wright experienced as enslaver after enslaver, upon learning he was a free man, found ways to prolong his enslavement, all while demanding Wright's ongoing cooperation. He must have been so very relieved to be home. He probably went to see his mother, Fanny, who lived in Philadelphia. He also made time to appear before the New York Vigilance Committee, which had used Wright's letter to James Hill to publicize his, Stephen Dickenson Jr.'s, and Robert Garrison's kidnapping and enslavement as well as worked to ensure their recovery. Although Isaac Wright and Stephen Dickenson Jr. eventually made their escape, I do not know what happened to Robert Garrison; I lose him in Arkansas. Isaac Wright's story, the one he knew to be true, was also an instrument used to secure his freedom. He was home. And while he may have no longer been under the thumb of men such as George Ann Botts, John McMahon, Hinson Gift, and John Simpson, that is not to say that Wright and his story were no longer of use or value to those who had enslaved him.[21]

In his capacity as curator of the estate of John McMahon, Robert Lawrence filed a lawsuit against George Ann Botts. According to Lawrence's attorneys, Peyton and Smith, on March 3, 1838, Botts sold McMahon a 21-year-old enslaved man named Isaac Wright for $1,050. However, unbeknownst to McMahon when he made his purchase, Wright "was then and had always been a free man." Lawrence's lawyers claimed that Botts had knowingly sold McMahon a free man and had thus acted "in bad faith and fraudulently." They then asked the court to order Botts to return the $1,050 sale price to McMahon's estate. To convince the court to rule in their client's favor, Peyton and Smith needed to prove that Botts had knowingly sold a free man to McMahon. In the process, they relied on the testimony of several witnesses, including Isaac Wright and his mother; Stephen Dickenson Jr. and his father, James Hill; and Joshua Coffin. In doing so, the lawyers made sure that Wright's story, even though he was no longer enslaved, was still of use to the estate of a man who had not only enslaved him but also worked to keep him in bondage after he discovered Wright was free.

On September 9, 1841, Wright was deposed in New York City. Did he want to testify? Did he feel as if he had a choice? How was the lawsuit described, if at all, to him? Did he know that his testimony would be used against George Ann Botts? Did he know that his testimony would be used to help John McMahon's estate? I wonder about the circumstances surrounding the deposition. I wonder how Wright felt about once more telling a story about his enslavement.

When Wright testified, he described the circumstances surrounding his kidnapping, enslavement, and subsequent escape in vivid detail. He also confirmed that George Ann Botts knew he was a free man when he sold him to John McMahon, corroborating Robert Lawrence's claims and playing an important role in the Orleans Parish Court's decision. On June 24, 1842, the jury ruled against Botts, ordering him to pay McMahon's estate the $1,050 that McMahon had paid for Wright along with an additional $500 in damages. The process of Isaac Wright's commodification and the value of what he had to say about the past did not cease when he made his escape from Tennessee in 1838; it culminated in his September 1841 testimony on behalf of his enslaver. His circumstances may have changed, but his history remained a site of his commodification.

There is no way to know how many stories about the past enslaved people like John were forced to memorize, practice, recite, and make sound believable. Isaac Wright's experiences provide us with a brief window into the coercive, violent methods enslavers used to compel the people they claimed as their enslaved property to perform their commodification. They also demonstrate how enslaved people's ability to reconstruct the past was an ongoing, evolving site of their exploitation and, sometimes, their emancipation. Isaac Wright fought, hard, to assemble the paper and ink necessary to communicate what was happening to him to those who could help him escape. Telling the truth, at specific moments and to certain people, was just as essential to his survival as deception.

Wright's experiences tell us that there were moments in enslaved people's lives when their history and their ability to convincingly reconstruct it was valuable, and that these moments shaped both the circumstances of their enslavement and the course of their lives in untold ways. The horrors that Wright and his companions endured bring into focus what some of those moments may have looked like for other enslaved people. In some ways, we are where we began, confronted with deliberately constructed archival walls that make a biography of enslaved people like John impossible to write. But Isaac Wright's story, and taking enslaved people's words seriously when and where we find them, get us somewhere else, too—somewhere closer to understanding how the enslaved, like their enslavers, brokered in information about themselves, revealing, concealing, and inventing parts of themselves and their pasts in the interest of their safety, security, and aspirations.

In his letter to the *Herald of Freedom*, published in the paper's March 7, 1835, issue, James L. Bradley, who was previously enslaved in Arkansas and South Carolina, wrote:

I know very well that slave-owners take a great deal of pains to make the people in the free States believe that the slaves are happy; but I know, likewise, that I was never acquainted with a slave, however well he was treated, who did not long to be free. There is one thing about this, that people in the free States do not understand. When they ask slaves whether they wish for their liberty, they answer, "No"; and very likely they will go so far as to say they would not leave their masters for the world. But at the same time, they desire liberty more than anything else, and have, perhaps, all along been laying plans to get free. The truth is, if a slave shows any discontent, he is sure to be treated worse, and worked the harder for it; and every slave knows this. This is why they are careful not to show any uneasiness when white men ask them about freedom. When they are alone by themselves, all their talk is about liberty—liberty! It is the great thought and feeling that fills the mind full all the time.[22]

James Bradley's words tell us that were moments when enslaved people knew they had to be "careful"; when they did what they could, when they could, to control and influence what they could, while prioritizing their survival. And when they were alone or with people they trusted, they could also find comfort in reflecting on the past or sharing their dearest hopes, dreams, and ambitions—parts of their lives that their enslavers, who so dominate the written record, were neither privy to nor cared to learn or write down. The consequences of enslavers' decisions and priorities shaped when and where the enslaved felt free to be themselves and to tell the truth; and these consequences reverberate in the stories we get to learn and tell now.

CHAPTER 3

Jack Smith

An Individual History and the Courtroom

Our responsibility to these vulnerable subjects is to
acknowledge and resist the perpetuation of their subjugation and commodification in our own discourse and
historical practices. It is a gesture toward redress.
—MARISA J. FUENTES, *Dispossessed Lives*

ON DECEMBER 31, 1853, Robert Hardin Marr filed a redhibition suit on
behalf of his client Alfred A. Williams in the Second District Court of
New Orleans. In his petition, Marr alleged that when Williams purchased an enslaved man named Jack Smith from William F. Talbot on
January 1, 1853, Williams was unaware that Smith was suffering from a
"certain incurable malady": "consumption." It was not until very recently, Marr went on, that Smith's illness had become apparent to his
owner, because it made it impossible for him to work. And as Talbot had
refused to take Smith back and return the $1,183 sale price, suing for red-
hibition was Williams's last chance to recoup his investment in a slave
he argued was useless.[1]

Robert Marr presented three pieces of documentary evidence to support his claims in court: an act of sale and two letters that his client
Williams sent to Talbot in 1853, informing him of Smith's declining
health and asking that Talbot issue a refund. But these documents alone
did not and could not establish cause for redhibition. Marr not only had
to explain that Smith was too sick to work but also had to prove, first,
that Smith had been too sick to work before Williams purchased him;
second, that Williams did not and could not have known about Smith's
illness when Williams bought Smith; and finally, that Williams had not

contributed to Smith's declining health since the date of sale. Marr thus needed to construct a historical narrative that centered on Jack Smith and moved forward and backward in time from the moment of sale.

During slave-centered redhibition suits, enslavers and their attorneys become historians of the enslaved, working to create a credible version of an enslaved person's past. The evidentiary requirements of these lawsuits combined with the limited availability of documentary evidence about enslaved individuals meant that plaintiffs could not necessarily win by fabricating a story about an unsound slave; they needed to construct and then corroborate—usually with testimony—a story about a *specific* enslaved person. Plaintiffs of course could and did use contracts to do some of that work, but because the evidence that was needed to establish cause for redhibition shifted depending on when a plaintiff filed suit and the nature of the complaint, contracts and the information contained therein could not always meet the burden of proof. And in the instances when their assertions and contracts alone were insufficient, enslavers and their lawyers turned to the enslaved.[2]

This chapter is about the last year of Jack Smith's life. It is also, necessarily, about what lawyers and witnesses said about him. Rather than summarize their arguments and testimony, I have endeavored to deconstruct the stories they told in court so as to reconstruct the extractive and exploitative practices that facilitated their construction. By suing for redhibition, Alfred A. Williams made the Second District Court of New Orleans into a site of historical production that centered on one enslaved man; records from *Williams v. Talbot* (1853) are not only our sole archival window into Smith's life, they are also the end result of Williams and his attorney's attempt to historicize Smith. When we consider how they were able to construct their history, we are left with a process that Jack Smith must have played an active role in.

Historicizing Jack Smith here and now is only possible because a man who owned him was invested in historicizing him in 1853. In this way, Smith is no different from the 332 enslaved people who found themselves at the center of 295 redhibition suits tried before the Orleans Parish Court. They too were sold in Louisiana, and at least 24 of them, like Smith, were led into courtrooms so that judges, juries, and witnesses could subject them to real-time, invasive appraisals.[3] But Jack Smith was unique in at least one way; to my knowledge, he is the only enslaved person who was transported to an out-of-state courtroom so that he could be present when individuals who were allowed to have their words preserved in the record responded to questions regarding his body and his past.[4]

This chapter is about Jack Smith, but it also stands to teach us something about the lives of other enslaved individuals. While historicizing Smith cannot tell every enslaved person's story, it does, first, reveal some of the strategies that enslavers relied on to extract important information from enslaved people. Second, it allows us to reach meaningful conclusions about how their efforts shaped the lives of the people they enslaved. And finally, it provides a road map for constructing histories of individuals who were meant to be historicized only as commodities.[5] Thus, working to learn about Jack Smith's life can help us make sense of the circumstances of enslavement that shaped and constrained the lives of others.

Williams v. Talbot (1853) is the first slave-centered redhibition suit I can remember reading. Jack Smith provided my first step into this world of lawsuits, evidence, and stories about the past. Over time, my approach to learning about him has changed. At first, I summarized what lawyers and witnesses said about him, and I took arguments and testimony as direct evidence of Smith's life. But summarizing the stories that free people told about Jack Smith in court cannot, on its own, help us learn about his life. It can only help us understand what stories were worth telling and recording in the world as it then was. Getting as close as we can to Smith's life requires that we move beyond summarizing court records and toward interrogating the production of these records. In this way—by asking questions about not just what was said but also what it may have been like to be the focus of what was said—we put ourselves in a position to acknowledge and critically interrogate the roles that enslaved people could and did play in the making of the past. I can never know whether what I have written here is a part of Jack Smith's life that he would have wanted told. I do, however, hope that it is a story he would have recognized.

A Sale

On January 1, 1853, Alfred A. Williams bought five enslaved people from William F. Talbot, as well as several more, whose names we do not know, from George Davis.[6] According to the bill of sale that Talbot penned and signed, the people Williams purchased were named Jack Smith, Logan Collins, John Smith, Terry Hayden, and Bright Smith. The sale took place at William Talbot's office, located at No. 7 Moreau Street, New Orleans; George Davis, who described himself as "long engaged in trade in slaves," managed a stand next door. When Davis was deposed in *Williams v. Talbot* (1853), he had little trouble remembering Jack Smith.[7]

As they stood outside Talbot's office door, Davis studied Smith's "chest, his arms and his hands. His hands," Davis would later recall, "were as hard as a board, showing that he had just come from work, and his muscles seemed as well developed as ever." During their 10-minute conversation, Davis testified, he never heard Smith "cough" or saw him "spit any blood." Based on this interaction, Davis "would have given six hundred dollars for [Smith] that day."[8]

There are at least two reasons to be skeptical of George Davis's description of Jack Smith. First, he arrived at his assessment by way of an invasive physical exam and interrogation. In those circumstances, it may have been in Smith's interest to neither cough nor divulge any information about a previous or existing illness, lest William Talbot overhear and reprimand him violently. Second, Davis, Talbot's neighbor and fellow slave trader, recounted his assessment under oath and during a civil suit in which he may have been invested in telling a story about Smith that would benefit Talbot's case. What we can be sure of is that Davis was in the business of appraising enslaved people. Whether or not he was honest about his conclusions regarding Smith, he was more than well acquainted with the process of extracting information from enslaved people's bodies and words so as to determine their soundness—so familiar, in fact, that he could certainly recite a plausible version of that process in court. He studied Jack Smith's hands and arms, carried on a brief discussion with him, and did the math in his head to determine what Smith was worth at the moment and could be worth in the future.[9]

None of the witnesses who testified in *Williams v. Talbot* (1853) discussed the other enslaved people whom Alfred A. Williams had purchased at any great length. We can gather their names and ages—at least the names and ages Williams and Talbot agreed to assign them—from the act of sale; and we can assume that as individuals Talbot intended to sell, they were subject to inspections and interrogations not so different from the one George Davis described in his testimony. The bill of sale that connects these enslaved individuals archivally gives us no insight into their respective paths to Talbot's New Orleans stand, which may have mirrored Jack Smith's in some ways or none at all.

Jack Smith was sold at least three times in 1852.[10] Each of these transactions, save for the last, kept him in the vicinity of Independence, Missouri, where he had probably been for the previous seven years.[11] In November 1852, Jabez Smith—a resident of Independence who was then the largest slaveholder in Missouri[12]—sold Jack Smith to John Mattingly.[13] According to another witness in *Williams v. Talbot* (1853), Mattingly, a slave trader who regularly purchased enslaved people in Kentucky and Missouri, had purchased Jack Smith "for a southern market."[14]

When it comes to understanding the relationships and practices of traders who left behind few, if any, personal papers, advertisements can be especially useful. John Mattingly began publishing advertisements in the *Louisville (KY) Daily Journal* as early as December 1848. In these ads, he regularly informed enslavers that he wished to purchase 100 enslaved people for "the highest cash prices."[15] The following year, in the same paper, William F. Talbot and his two partners advertised a $300 reward for Henry Buchanan and John Scott, two enslaved men who had absconded. If anyone should apprehend Henry or John, the ad read, they should "address our agent, Mr. John Mattingly, of Lexington, Kentucky."[16]

If John Mattingly was acting as William F. Talbot's agent when he purchased Jack Smith in November 1853, then Smith, at least legally, came into Talbot's possession when Mattingly purchased him. Between

September and December of 1852, William Talbot advertised, in New Orleans's *Daily Picayune*, 150 enslaved people who had "just arrived" and were available for sale at his "old stand," located at no. 7 Moreau Street. The ad described those for sale as "likely" and "consisting of field hands, house servants and mechanics."[17] Although Jack Smith would not have arrived in New Orleans until November or December 1852, those whom Talbot sold to Alfred Williams along with Smith may have already been in New Orleans when he arrived; it is also possible that they made the journey southward from Missouri with Smith. Regardless of how their paths converged in the Crescent City, at least one facet of their journey was the same: on January 1, 1853, William F. Talbot sold Jack Smith, Logan Collins, John Smith, Terry Hayden, and Bright Smith to Alfred A. Williams for a total of $5,858. They were then transported to Williams's plantation in Baton Rouge just two days later. Save for the one, unnamed person among them whom Williams returned to Talbot due to a "defect of sight" some 30 or 40 days after the sale, this is where we lose Logan Collins, John Smith, Terry Hayden, and Bright Smith.[18]

Alfred A. Williams's lawsuit inserted the people he purchased from William F. Talbot into the written record, albeit briefly; and while Jack Smith's experiences before and after the sale creates a space for us to speculate that some of the experiences of those purchased alongside him could have been much the same, we have no way of knowing that for certain. To speculate further, when Smith became the focus of a redhibition suit, those sold alongside him in New Orleans may have been asked questions about him, by Alfred Williams or someone in his employ. If Williams thought Jack, Bright, and John's shared last name indicated a common previous owner, Bright and John may have been asked to disclose information about themselves and their pasts as they related to Jack Smith. The nature of records from *Williams v. Talbot* (1853) are such that anything we might wonder or attempt to reasonably conclude about John Smith, Bright Smith, Terry Hayden, and Logan Collins makes sense only in relation to Jack Smith. Court records from redhibition suits can be windows into an enslaved person's past, to be sure, but they are not all-seeing.

In November 1853, Alfred A. Williams sent a letter to William F. Talbot, informing him that Jack Smith was "consumptive, and was so before the sale and even before you [Talbot] bought him. The overseer who has charge of him," Williams continued, "has had charge of him ever since I got him [and] hoped all along that it was only a common cold and would gradually wear off, using mild remedies during the spring and summer, and suffering him to do what he thought himself able as he had orders from me to take extraordinary care of all of them for a year." He explained that Smith had been seen by two physicians and, because of his illness, had "not done anything" for a lengthy period; further, as he was "hoping to cure him up," Williams "had a place fixed for him over the sugar kettles where he may inhale the vapor, and feed him from my table and do all that I can for him." After attempting to convince Talbot that he could give him his money back and still fetch a high price for Smith, Williams turned to the subject of a potential lawsuit. Such proceedings, he wrote, "would be troublesome, annoying and expensive to both of us," and "I believe," he continued, "I can procure the affidavit of a gentleman who knows that Jack has had this cough two years ago."[19]

Alfred Williams had a lawsuit on his mind when he wrote to William Talbot. In keeping a copy of his letter, a copy that Robert Marr, Williams's attorney, would later present to the Second District Court, Williams was creating evidence, and he knew it. To establish cause for redhibition, Marr needed to prove that Williams had done everything in his power to treat Jack Smith's illness and had in no way contributed to its development. Thus, Williams's assertions about the "extraordinary care" Smith received, as well as the minimal work he was expected to do and the food he was given from Williams's table, were probably more in line with the story his lawyer might need to tell in court than with the actual circumstances of Smith's enslavement in 1853. What's more, Williams's final, looming threat of an affidavit from an unnamed source who could testify that Smith had been consumptive two years earlier indicates that he had already started looking for evidence elsewhere.

While the act of sale that William Talbot penned and signed as well as the letters Alfred Williams sent to Talbot in November 1853 could help Robert Marr build his case, they could not, on their own, establish cause for redhibition. As an enslaved man, Jack Smith could not serve as a witness in court, but that did not stop Williams and his lawyer from looking to him for the information they needed to build their case. While they could rely on men in Williams's employ, including overseers and physicians, to testify that Smith had become increasingly ill as Williams did his best to treat him, they also needed to locate witnesses who could testify that they had seen Smith fail to work because of his illness *before* Williams purchased him. But first, they needed to know where to look.

Questions

On April 17, 1854, A. J. Villere sent a letter addressed to John W. Reid, J. B. Hovey, Charles H. Thornton, or "any Judge or Justice of the Peace in Jackson County, Missouri." Villere, a clerk for the Second District Court of New Orleans, expressed the court's "reposing confidence" in the "prudence and fidelity" of Jackson County's judges and justices of the peace before requesting they examine several witnesses on behalf of the plaintiff in *Williams v. Talbot* (1853). Along with his letter, Villere included two sets of questions, one from Robert Hardin Marr, Alfred Williams's attorney, and the other from William F. Talbot's lawyers, Edward Warren Moise and W. M. Randolph. The questions were intended for America Palmer, Daniel D. White, Lewis Sharp, Sally Handley Fisher, Robert G. Smart, and "others residing in the neighborhood of Independence in Jackson County, State of Missouri."[20]

Looking outside Louisiana's borders for potential witnesses in a slave-centered redhibition suit was not unusual. Redhibition suits could easily become interstate affairs, especially when an enslaved person had recently been transported across state lines. Redhibition suits tried before the Orleans Parish Court included such cases as *Keys v. Brown* (1834), which involved a witness from Onondaga, New York; *Chabert v. Deverges Jr.* (1832), in which witnesses from South Carolina were deposed; and *Layson v. Boudar* (1845), in which witnesses from Maryland, North Carolina, the District of Columbia, and Virginia testified.[21] Because Jack Smith had spent much of the previous decade enslaved on farms in northwestern Missouri, deposing out-of-state witnesses was not simply a strategy Robert Marr chose to employ; it was also the only way he could build his case.

Of the five individuals named in A. J. Villere's letter, only three testified in *Williams v. Talbot* (1853): America Palmer, Daniel D. White, and Robert G. Smart.[22] When Palmer and White testified on May 5, 1853, they responded to two sets of questions, the first, from Robert Marr, and the second, from Edward Moise and W. M. Randolph. Because the lawyers were sending their questions to a Missouri official who would interview the witnesses on their behalf, all strove to be as clear as possible. What follows are Moise and Randolph's set of questions in their entirety:

> 1st State your age and your occupation. State how long you have known Jack "or" jack Smith where did you first see him and where? Has he ever been in your service, if yes how long and what labor did he perform, or what was the general character of his occupation where you knew him. If you answer to the chief interrogatories that he has been sick state fully particularly and minutely the nature and general character of his disease? State what was the nature and character of the disease with which he was affected. Did he recover from it?

> 2nd State particularly how you know that the slave which is the subject of this suit is the same slave of whose health you answer in the interrogatories in chief and especially state the facts and circumstances from which you form your opinion.

> 3rd Do you know defendant? How do you know that he is the owner of the Slave of whose health you have answered. Is the fact known to you personally or do you not believe it because you have been so informed by others.[23]

These questions demonstrate that William F. Talbot's attorneys were attempting to poke holes in the Missouri witnesses' testimony. If the attorneys could cast doubt on whatever information they had about Jack Smith, they could undermine Alfred Williams's claims about a long-standing illness. Whereas their first set of questions were meant to establish what the witnesses knew about Jack Smith, the second took aim at how they could be certain that the enslaved person they were describing was the same enslaved person at the center of *Williams v. Talbot* (1853). Their questions were *exactly* what almost every attorney representing a defendant in a slave-centered redhibition suit asked witnesses who claimed to have knowledge about an enslaved person:

What do you know?
How do you know it?
How can you be sure that the person you're describing is the same
    person at the center of this lawsuit?

Robert Marr's questions were extensive and more detailed. Because it was Marr who requested that specific witnesses in Missouri be deposed, we can assume that he had good reason to believe their testimony would benefit his case. His questions, which are transcribed in their entirety here, tell a story all their own:

First. State your age residence and occupation.

Second. Do you know anything of a negro named Jack "or Jack Smith," formerly the property of Nathan Harroldson? If you do, State where you saw him first, in whose possession he was, when and where you saw him last, in whose possession he then was, and whether or not you recognize the Jack that you saw last, as the same Jack you saw first.

Third. Since you have known Jack has his health always been uniformly good? If it has not State what sickness he has had to your knowledge, does it affected him, how long he was sick, and whether his attack was violent or mild in its character.

Fourth. was or not the negro Jack whom you speak of once the property of Fisher, the husband now deceased of Mrs. Sally Handley Fisher? If he was from whom did Fisher buy him? Did or not Fisher return the negro to the person from whom he purchased him? If he did return him, State the cause and when this was.

Fifth. It is alleged that the negro in controversy was purchased by Talbot of one Jabez Smith of Independence, or of that vicinity. State if you knew from whom Smith bought him.

Sixth. This Suit is brought to recover the price paid for Jack on the ground that he has a certain incurable disease, viz the consumption State any fact coming within your knowledge going to show what is the truth with regard to this Statement and State also your means of knowing whatever you do State.

Seventh. State any fact within your knowledge going to show that the negro bought by Williams of Talbott is the same negro once sold by Harroldson to Fisher and the same negro about whose health you have testified Also state your means of knowing that he is the same. Where you saw that negro last, by whom he was shown to you, for what purpose, and in whose possession he was at the time he was so shown to you.[24]

Robert Marr prodded his carefully selected witnesses to tell a story he already knew and believed they could recite. He mentioned three of Jack Smith's previous owners by name, including Nathan E. Harrelson, Richard Fisher, and Jabez Smith. Marr also recounted a specific instance when Smith had been purchased and returned. If we work backward from Edward Warren Moise and W. M. Randolph's questions—asking how they went about constructing them and where they obtained the information necessary to do so—we arrive at Louisiana's redhibition laws and the arguments Marr made in his petition. But their questions contained few details about Jack Smith; save for using Smith's name, Moise and Randolph's questions would not have been out of place in any redhibition suit wherein the plaintiff alleged that an enslaved person was too sick to be of any use. When we work backward from Robert Marr's questions, however, we arrive at information that was unique to Jack Smith. Marr did not simply ask the Missouri witnesses what they knew about Smith; he also described specific instances when Smith had been bought, sold, and returned because he was too sick to work. What's more, Marr designed his questions for five specific individuals, none of whom was among Smith's previous owners or had any discernible relationship with Alfred Williams. By including such detailed information in his questions, Robert Marr betrayed much in the way of how he located the Missouri witnesses and how he knew what to ask them. If someone had asked Marr from whom he gathered all the details in his questions, and if he were inclined to tell the truth, he might have answered, "Jack Smith."

Between January 1, 1853, and April 17, 1854—the day the Second District Court of New Orleans clerk sent two sets of questions to Independence, Missouri—Jack Smith was interrogated. Robert Marr's questions demonstrate that he had some knowledge about Smith's life in Missouri, but they tell us precious little about how he acquired it. Taking a closer look at those who testified on Alfred Williams's behalf in Louisiana, however, allows us to come to some important conclusions about what the process of gathering that information may have looked like.

By 1850, Alfred Augustus Williams owned approximately 130 enslaved people.[25] He engaged in both cotton and sugar production on his sizable holdings, located on either side of the Mississippi River in East and West Baton Rouge Parishes. With so many enslaved people on his properties, it is unlikely that Williams was in the habit of regularly interacting with every person he owned; he had overseers to do that for him.[26]

William F. J. Davis, a 27-year-old white man, worked as an overseer on Alfred Williams's East Baton Rouge sugar plantation. He was also the only witness who testified about Jack Smith's life between January and October 1853. Davis recalled first seeing Smith in January of that year, when he "landed at the plantation of A. A. Williams." Two or three weeks later, Davis would later testify, he "discovered that Jack was afflicted with a bad cough"; his discovery by no means kept him from putting Smith to work. According to Davis, save for driving a bagasse cart for a week during rolling season and "working the kettles for three or four days, chopping wood" was the only work Jack Smith was employed at on the plantation up to the middle of October 1853.[27] And while Smith "frequently failed in getting his task owing to weakness," Davis testified, "Jack was never punished for not getting his task" nor was he ever "unusually exposed to the wet and cold."[28]

As an overseer, William Davis's job was to make sure that the men, women, and children whom Alfred Williams owned did theirs. By the 1850s, American enslavers with plantations as vast as Williams's were well practiced in violently managing enslaved people. Such practices involved employing men who, quite literally, oversaw the enslaved. While Davis's individual strategies remain obscured from our view, those that other enslaved people experienced at the hands of overseers are well documented.[29] Frederick Douglass remembered a man by the name of Austin Gore who possessed "all those traits of character indispensable to what is called a first-rate overseer." He was not only "proud, ambitious, and preserving" but also "artful, cruel, and obdurate." "Mr. Gore acted fully up to the maxim laid down by slaveholders," Douglass continued: "It is better that a dozen slaves suffer under the lash, than that the overseer should be convicted, in the presence of slaves, of having been at fault." Austin Gore "was cruel enough to inflict the severest punishment, artful enough to descend to the lowest trickery, and obdurate enough to be insensible to the voice of a reproving conscience. He was, of all the overseers, the most dreaded by the slaves. His presence was painful; his eye flashed confusion; and seldom was his sharp, shrill voice heard without producing horror and trembling in their ranks."[30]

William Davis did not hear Jack Smith cough and lighten his workload; instead, as Alfred Williams likely expected, he may have employed violence and coercion to force Smith to work as much as he could. Williams left behind no personal papers, but what we know about Louisiana sugar planters tells us much about the kinds of labor that Williams and his overseers demanded of the enslaved. When he arrived in East Baton Rouge in January 1853, Jack Smith may have been forced to help plant sugarcane that would not be harvested until October, but, of course, there would have been much work to do other than planting and harvesting. Enslaved people maintained drainage canals and levees year-round; they constantly dug out the weeds that grew around the cane, produced other crops for sustenance, and chopped wood. During grinding season, which began in October, they cut cane at the root, stripped the leaves, and transported the crop to the mill. There, they extracted sugar juice through an evaporation process that involved four open kettles and a roaring furnace.[31] It was there, at Williams's sugar house in the middle of grinding season, that Dr. Louis Favrot first encountered Jack Smith.

Dr. Favrot was one of five physicians who testified on Alfred Williams's behalf; he was also Williams's neighbor, and he treated Jack Smith on at least two occasions, once in October and again in November 1853.[32] According to Dr. Favrot, he was not invited to Williams's East Baton Rouge plantation to examine Smith, but while the physician was on the property, Smith's cough caught his attention. He found Jack Smith "exposed like all the other hands about the sugar house, and upon further inspection, he discovered that Smith was suffering from fever, and," the doctor testified, "the boy informed the witness that he had fever every night." The physician subsequently told Williams and his overseer that Smith "was more sick than they appeared to think he was," prescribed some medicine, and returned three weeks later to examine Smith just once more. After inspecting some of Williams's other slaves in West Baton Rouge, Favrot "was requested" to take a look at Smith and "found him in the same situation as when he first saw him."[33]

Smith was forced to work on Williams's sugar plantation throughout much of 1853. William Davis's testimony that Smith worked for only a few days was, in all likelihood, an outright lie. Dr. Louis Favrot heard Smith cough in October, and while it was severe enough to attract a doctor's attention, it had not yet convinced the overseer that Smith was too sick to work. When Favrot returned to examine Smith the following month, the physician found him "in the same situation," suggesting that by November 1853, neither an enduring cough nor a doctor's advice could prevent Alfred Williams and William Davis from forcing Jack Smith to work.

November 1853 was the last time Dr. Louis Favrot saw Jack Smith, but judging from his testimony, it was probably not the first time he had been asked to treat the people whom Alfred Williams claimed as his enslaved property. Plaintiffs in slave-centered redhibition suits, especially those whose claims centered on illnesses, often had physicians testify on their behalf. Calling a doctor to the stand could support plaintiff's cases in two ways: first, it could demonstrate that they had invested both money and resources in treating the enslaved individual in question; and second, doctors could historicize an illness, arguing that a specific condition must have existed well before a sale took place.[34] And while doctors who examined enslaved people at an owner's behest surely provided treatment, we should not lose sight of the fact that these men were appraisers, invested in extracting information from the enslaved long before they set foot inside a courtroom. The honorific *Dr.* may have preceded their names, but on the ground, such physicians were not so different from overseers, working for a slaveowner and toward a shared goal of ensuring that an enslaved person was sound.[35]

Enslavers dug for information and created it when it was valuable for them to do so. Jack Smith's health and ability to work had not suddenly become important to Alfred Williams when Robert Marr submitted a petition to the Second District Court of New Orleans; Smith's soundness mattered to Williams from the moment Smith became Williams's property on January 1, 1853. Just two days after the sale, Smith was working under the watchful eye of William Davis. His health and his ability to work definitely mattered to Williams then, but it mattered more, or at least received a different kind of attention, after Dr. Louis Favrot noticed Jack's cough.

Jack Smith was interrogated. Someone, and likely more than one person, asked him questions about himself. As an enslaved man, he would have been accustomed to being on the receiving end of requests that sounded more like demands; he would have known how to weigh potential responses, straining to produce an answer that might ward off punishment or yield a result he desired; and he would have known what it was like to give the wrong one. By the time Alfred Williams decided to sue William Talbot for redhibition, whoever was in the habit of asking Smith questions would have begun prying into his past and asked him not only how he was feeling but also how long he had been feeling that way. The interrogator would have prodded Smith into historicizing his cough, rooting its existence in 1852, if not earlier. The interrogator also would have encouraged Smith to recount previous instances when he had tried to work and failed because he was sick. And the interrogator would have insisted that Smith disclose the names of his former owners and any free individuals who could describe his illness in court. Information about Jack Smith had not *recently* become of interest to Alfred Williams. The focus and aim of that interest had merely shifted.

The information that Smith had about himself and his past was valuable to Williams, and he may have used violence and coercion or even promises of potential rewards to get it. But that would not have made it into the records of the Second District Court, as any hint of violence directed at Smith would have undermined Williams's claim. Thus, the precise circumstances surrounding the interrogations conducted in the interest of winning a lawsuit—not in the interest of assessing whether Smith could work on Williams's sugar plantation—remain deliberately elusive. We are also left to speculate whether whoever interrogated Smith explained why they were asking such questions. If Smith was in the dark, he may have found the answers to many of his questions at the Jackson County Courthouse.

Answers

Jack Smith met James Wallace for the first time on April 12, 1854. At the time, Smith was sick and lying in bed somewhere on Alfred A. Williams's West Baton Rouge property. Wallace, a 25-year-old white man, was then living and working on Williams's stock farm in East Baton Rouge. He had been summoned to West Baton Rouge by his employer, who had instructed him to transport Smith to Independence. The trip, Wallace would later testify, was "for the purposes of ascertaining whether the boy was diseased previous to the purchase of [Alfred] Williams and for the purpose of identifying the boy as the one purchased by Talbot."[36]

Wallace and Smith set out for Independence, Missouri, on April 13, 1854. From West Baton Rouge, they headed for New Orleans, where they boarded the *Peter Tellon*, a steamboat bound for Missouri, probably on the evening of April 18, 1854.[37] The *Peter Tellon* was an 800-ton side-wheel steamboat constructed especially for the New Orleans trade. It regularly carried passengers and cargo—including sugar, cotton, tobacco, whiskey, lard, corn, and flour—from New Orleans and up the Mississippi, making stops in Louisville, Kentucky, and St. Louis, Missouri.[38] Despite James Wallace's testimony to the contrary, Jack Smith was in all likelihood confined to the steamboat's deck throughout the voyage. He would have slept outside in the wet and the cold, among other enslaved people, the ship's cargo, and the poorest passengers.[39] On May 5, after what was no doubt a trying journey for Smith, he and Wallace finally arrived in Independence.

The details that consistently emerged in Robert Marr's questions and several witnesses' testimony can help us outline, albeit broadly, certain aspects of Jack Smith's time in Missouri. America Palmer remembered first seeing "the boy Jack" at the home of her daughter, Sally Handley Fisher, and son-in-law, Richard Fisher, in the spring of 1845 or 1846, but she could not remember exactly where or when Richard purchased Jack.[40] To her, he looked "healthy and sprightly." Daniel D. White, who met Jack at around the same time, "thought him unhealthy," telling his wife, Lucy, that "he would like to own him if he was sound" but did not believe he was. White, a slaveowner and farmer, thought himself a "good judge of the general health of slaves," and had he been interested in purchasing any enslaved people at the time, he "would not have bought [Jack Smith] for a sound negro."[41]

Even if Jack Smith did not share Daniel White's opinion, he may have believed that such an assessment was worth sharing with Richard Fisher. Soon after Fisher purchased him, Smith informed his new owner that he was "not sound nor strong," a comment Fisher subsequently shared with his mother-in-law. Together, Fisher; his wife, Sally; and America Palmer discussed Smith's remark, arriving at the conclusion that he had described himself as unsound in an attempt to manipulate Fisher "because he did not want to be sold." Several months later, Fisher and his family would ultimately come to agree with Smith's self-appraisal.[42]

That summer, Fisher sent Smith to help raise "a heaved log house" at Daniel White's farm, also located in Independence. Smith worked alongside some 10 or 12 other enslaved men before he started "spitting blood and continued to do so for about an hour." White watched him cough up blood, waited until he decided Smith was well enough to walk, and finally sent him back to Fisher's farm. The next time he saw Smith, White thought he "looked badly," "puny and weakly." America Palmer, who witnessed Smith experience a similar "violent" attack, supposed it was caused by a hemorrhage of the lungs; and although she and a local physician endeavored to treat him, Smith was scarcely able to work on Fisher's farm from then on.

Two men testified that they were present when Fisher returned Smith to his previous owner, but they told different stories, and neither mentioned the other. Freeman McKinney, who worked for Fisher in Independence but had since moved to San Jose, California, said that he had accompanied Fisher to return Smith at the end of February 1846; Daniel White, however, claimed "he was present when he [Richard Fisher] delivered [Jack Smith] back to the said Nathan E. Harrelson" and that the "cause assigned for Fisher's delivering said slave back and for Harrelson's taking him back was admitted by both of them to be the ill health or unsoundness of said slave."[43]

It is possible that Jack Smith remained in Nathan Harrelson's possession until 1852. Robert Marr's questions as well as Jacob Hall's testimony indicate that it was Harrelson who sold Smith to Hall in the spring or summer of that year. By the 1850s, Harrelson was one of the largest landowners in Cass County, Missouri. He owned a dry goods store and regularly bought and sold land in northwestern Missouri, and he surely could have exploited Smith in any one of these ventures.[44] Hall, a farmer and attorney, testified that Smith worked on his Independence hemp farm as both a carpenter and a farmhand between May and November 1852, when he ultimately sold Smith to Jabez Smith, who subsequently sold him to John Mattingly, a slave trader who may have been acting as William F. Talbot's agent at the time.[45]

While we cannot know precisely when Richard Fisher returned Jack Smith to his previous owner, I am fairly certain that by the time he arrived in Baton Rouge, Smith knew what it felt like to be sold and found wanting. When Robert Marr asked America Palmer and Daniel White whether "Fisher return[ed] the negro to the person who purchased him," Marr already knew the answer; but it was Palmer's and White's affirmation that he required. He depended on Jack Smith's willingness to disclose information about his past to help him locate witnesses such as Palmer and White—individuals whose connection to Smith could never have been deciphered archivally, as neither had ever bought, sold, or mortgaged him—because however rooted in reality Smith's memories were, as an enslaved man, he could never recite them in the space of a courtroom. His lived experiences could be exploited only if they were narrated by free men and women who did not see him as a sick man in need of help and compassion but as an unsound slave. Robert Marr believed Jack Smith; he demonstrated his faith with every witness he called on and each question he asked them. And while I am confident in America Palmer's and Daniel White's story about Richard Fisher purchasing Smith and ultimately deciding to return him, I have deemed them credible for two reasons: Smith told that story first, and Palmer and White had nothing to lose by telling it in court.[46]

When Jack Smith was interrogated in Louisiana, he was asked questions about his health and his previous owners, and, in response, he told stories about not only himself and his cough but also free individuals who had borne witness to what must have been difficult, even terrifying moments for him. He named names, those of the men who had previously owned him as well as their neighbors, employees, and family members. The out-of-state witnesses whom Robert Marr called on to testify hint at just how expansive Smith's world in Missouri must have been. Of course, he may have told other stories too, stories that involved precious memories of loved ones whom he did not dare hope to see again; but those would not have been of interest to Robert Marr and Alfred Williams and thus remain obscured from our view.

Jack Smith's experiences provide us with significant insight into a world where interrogation was among enslavers' tools. It is important to note, however, that enslavers' invasive maneuvers did not always cease once an enslaved person passed away. For some enslaved people, their bodies remained valuable sources of information, even in death. And in these instances, once more, enslavers turned to physicians for help.

On April 7, 1831, an enslaved child named Aggy was sold in New Orleans. When the day started, she was the property of Garland Tate, a white man from Campbell County, Virginia, and by the day's end, she was claimed by Adele Giraudeau, a free woman of color and resident of New Orleans. According to Giraudeau's lawyer, less than three days after the sale, "Aggy appeared to be unwell." Upon further inspection, likely by a physician, Giraudeau learned that Aggy was suffering from a "chronic disease of the lungs." Aggy's condition did not improve, and she passed away on September 16, 1831. Two months later, Giraudeau sued Tate for redhibition in the Orleans Parish Court.

After Aggy died, or perhaps as she was dying, Adele Giraudeau hired two physicians to conduct an autopsy. On September 17, the day after Aggy died, they cut open her chest. They put their hands inside her lungs. They chatted among themselves as they looked for signs of disease. And they ultimately concluded that Aggy suffered and died from consumption. Later, at Adele Giraudeau's request, the doctors testified before the Orleans Parish Court, describing their "inspection" and conclusions in vivid detail. Giraudeau had charged the physicians with not only prying information from Aggy's body but also constructing a plausible historical narrative in court, one that placed the origins of Aggy's illness well before Giraudeau made her purchase. One final time, an enslaver demanded that Aggy divulge information about herself and her past. Giraudeau must have thought the $10 she paid each physician was well spent, with one testifying that based on the condition of Aggy's lungs, she was sick for at least five or six years before the sale. They told the story Giraudeau needed them to tell, and we are left with the story they told.[47]

Aggy was not a willing participant in the story Adele Giraudeau and her lawyer worked to tell in court. Aggy's body divulged information when she did not have the consciousness necessary to consent or actively participate. Nevertheless, her body remained a site of her commodification. In life, Aggy's body was subject to invasive inspections and appraisals as well. And it is important to note that even with consciousness and unwillingness, one's body could still reveal information. Did Jack Smith's body ever betray him? Did he ever cough or trip when he meant to breathe evenly and stand up straight? As enslavers delved for information, we cannot lose sight of the fact that enslaved people were simultaneously working to tell a certain story about themselves, too, to hide parts of themselves and their pasts while showing or inventing others. In these endeavors, one's body was an important part of the story one told—though perhaps not always a consistent or deliberate part.

On May 9, 1854, four days after arriving in Independence, Jack Smith and James Wallace made their way to the Jackson County Courthouse. As Smith had spent much of the previous decade enslaved on farms within miles of the two-story, steepled building, the sight before them probably looked more familiar to him than to Wallace. On that Tuesday morning, America Palmer, Daniel D. White, and Robert G. Smart also made their way to the courthouse, and they exchanged words with Wallace and Smith before they entered the building. As Palmer and White were sworn and deposed before Jackson County Commissioner J. Brown Harvey, Smith and Wallace looked on, listening as a white man and a white woman responded to two sets of questions.

Robert G. Smart did not testify on May 9, 1854; he was deposed on August 25 of that year. Nevertheless, the fact that he had recognized Jack Smith three months earlier played an important part in his testimony, as he explained, "Jack was present at the time Mr. White and Mrs. Palmer were examined as witnesses."[48] At the time, Smart continued, he thought Smith "looked badly used up, looked thin and emaciated," and he was "evidently in very bad health." Judging from America Palmer's and Daniel White's testimony, they were left with much the same impression. When responding to Robert Marr's second set of questions,[49] Palmer answered as follows:

I first saw the boy Jack at the house of Richard Fisher my son in law now deceased about the spring of 1845 or 6. This boy was at said Fisher's in Jackson County Missouri from Spring till late in the fall, and I now at this day recognize the boy Jack from his conversation more than from his personal appearance, he answers all my questions correctly as to matters transpiring in the family of said Fisher and relating to matters which no person unacquainted or not intimate with our family could possibly have answered correctly, and I have no doubt that the boy Jack now here in the possession of Mr. Wallace now before me while testifying, is the same slave which I saw first at Fisher's. I should not have recognized the boy at this time by his personal appearance but he rehearsed particularly all the events transpiring in our family at the time he was there, which no person could do unless he had lived in our family.[50]

America Palmer barely recognized Jack Smith when she saw him in May 1854. Almost a year and a half in Baton Rouge followed by a long journey up the Mississippi must have taken their toll. He was sick, he was dying, and he must have looked it. Had he been unwilling to answer Palmer's questions, her testimony may have been very different. And what answers might Smith have given if he had not been under the watchful eye of James Wallace? Any reluctance to respond or enthusiastically engage with Palmer and White would almost certainly have been met with a violent reprisal. And yet, Smith made a choice to participate in another interrogation. He had been taken to Missouri to perform, and he decided to perform as Alfred Williams and James Wallace demanded.

Williams paid Wallace to transport Smith to the Jackson County Courthouse so as to undermine any argument that William Talbot's attorneys hoped to make about the discrepancies between the enslaved man the Missouri witnesses would describe in their testimony and the enslaved man at the center of *Williams v. Talbot* (1853). Smith was not taken to Independence to testify under oath, but his informed responses were nevertheless essential to America Palmer's and Daniel White's testimony. His presence in that courtroom and his willingness to respond to their questions outside the courthouse on that Tuesday morning made their claims—and by extension, Robert Marr's and Alfred Williams's—more credible.

Neither Williams nor Marr would have sent Jack Smith to Independence if they did not believe it would help them establish cause for redhibition. And if we are to count violent punishments among the possibilities that crossed Smith's mind as he made his way to Missouri and eventually stood outside the Jackson County Courthouse, we must also consider that the journey may have been reason enough to cooperate. According to America Palmer and Daniel White, Smith had been enslaved on farms in Jackson County since at least 1845 or 1846. It is thus possible that there were enslaved people, family and friends, in Independence whom he hoped to see once more. As he arrived in town on May 5—four days before Palmer and White were deposed—we can choose to imagine, albeit hopefully, that sometime during those four days, Smith experienced a joyful reunion, or even several, that he believed impossible when he was sold southward to New Orleans in November 1852.

Jack Smith and James Wallace returned to Alfred Williams's plantation in West Baton Rouge Parish on May 20 or 21, 1854. Dr. J. A. Cassot, who had examined Smith just before the journey, continued treating him after he arrived. "At that time," Dr. Cassot would testify almost three months later, "the cough was very troublesome, the expectoration very profuse, the night sweats copious, the strength greatly reduced, and diarrhea constant." He managed Smith's diet and continued to treat him over the next few weeks, but his health continued to deteriorate. He developed bedsores and, Dr. Cassot explained, "his symptoms went on increasing with very little mitigation." By the time Smith passed away in mid-June 1854, the doctor thought him reduced to a "perfect living skeleton."[51]

Alfred Williams's attempt to recoup his investment in Jack Smith continued for another two years after Smith's death.[52] On April 21, 1856, Judge P. H. Morgan issued a verdict in favor of the defendant, William F. Talbot. That same day, Robert Marr filed an appeal on Williams's behalf. After reviewing the case and hearing arguments, Louisiana Supreme Court Justice James Lawrence Cole explained the higher court's decision in three short pages. He found fault with "the neglect of [the] plaintiff to send for aid for so many months after the first manifestation of symptoms of disease." It was Williams's "neglect" that convinced the Louisiana Supreme Court to "bar his action of redhibition." Justice Cole was also unconvinced by the testimony of the physicians who attempted to root Jack Smith's illness well in his past. The fact that Williams had not called a doctor when Smith's cough first revealed itself rendered any evidence the physicians provided "nugatory." If "the witnesses had been called at the first opening of the malady," Justice Cole reasoned, then they could have testified regarding the origins and development of Smith's illness, but because none of the five physicians who testified on Williams's behalf were called when Smith's cough first appeared, none could state for certain that his disease was not neglected or incurable before Williams purchased him. Ultimately, Justice Cole decided that it was of no consequence whether Smith had suffered from an incurable disease. "Even if it could be proved," he wrote, "this would not be of itself sufficient to cancel a sale, for if a physician called at the primary manifestation of the disease, the life of the slave might have been extended for some years." In the end, the courts found fault with Alfred Williams, not because Jack Smith died, but because Williams had not made efficient use of him while he was alive. With that, the Louisiana Supreme Court reaffirmed the lower court's decision.[53]

Robert Marr and Alfred Williams depended on Jack Smith to help them establish cause for redhibition. In a space where he could neither speak nor have his words documented, Smith was essential, which is precisely why, even though we cannot take what witnesses and lawyers said about him at face value, we can dissect their statements so as to reconstruct the processes of extraction, historicization, and commodification that shaped Smith's life and constrained his choices. Such an analysis not only illuminates the circumstances of Smith's enslavement but also allows us to find traces of his lived experiences. That is not to say that what I have written here is the story Jack Smith would have wanted told; such assurances cannot be found in court records. It is only to say that it becomes impossible to write enslaved people out of our histories when we acknowledge that their enslavers never wrote them out of theirs.

CHAPTER 4

Transforming Betsey into Rachel

Oh! how heavily the weight of slavery pressed upon me
then. I must toil day after day, endure abuse and taunts
and scoffs, sleep on the hard ground, live on the coarsest
fare, and not only this, but live the slave of a blood-
seeking wretch, of whom I must stand henceforth in
continued fear and dread. . . . I sighed for liberty; but the
bondsman's chain was round me, and could not be shaken
off. I could only gaze wistfully toward the North, and
think of the thousands of miles that stretched between me
and the soil of freedom, over which a *black* freeman may
not pass.

—SOLOMON NORTHUP, *Twelve Years a Slave*

SHE CALLED HERSELF BETSEY, but he called her Rachel. Court records
from the freedom suit she filed later, in June 1819, tell us he went by the
name Cage. They also tell us that he was hired by a man named Joseph
Erwin to arrest her as Erwin's enslaved property. Of course, she had no
way of knowing that when Cage approached her in New Orleans's Faubourg St. Mary neighborhood. To her, he may have seemed to be just
another imposing, entitled white man, demanding both information
and submission. As Cage meant to arrest her, he may have put his hands
on her so as to prevent her from fleeing. But even if he did not move to
physically restrain her, I suspect their interaction inspired fear, panic,
and dread. Here was a man, calling her a slave, and here she was, without any means of escaping or proving she was a free woman named
Betsey, not an enslaved woman named Rachel.[1]

The arrest was not unusual in the context of antebellum New Orleans. As John Bardes demonstrates in his meticulous study of arrests in Orleans Parish, "New Orleans' police jails confined and tortured hundreds of free Black sailors and transient workers, each year, on the pretext that they were captured runaway slaves."[2] The fact that Betsey subsequently filed a freedom suit, however, makes her unique. *Betsey alias Rachel v. St. Amand* (1819) is one of sixty-one freedom suits tried before the Orleans Parish Court between 1813 and 1846. This means that of the 17,006 civil suits tried before the court during that period, only 61 were lawsuits wherein an enslaved person or persons claimed that they were entitled to their freedom. It was difficult for the enslaved to gain access to New Orleans's courts. What, then, are we to make of the records left behind by those who did?

A plaintiff in a freedom suit, not unlike a plaintiff in a redhibition suit, was also a kind of historian. Both relied on written evidence and witness testimony to construct a compelling historical narrative. But unlike the dissatisfied buyers who filed redhibition suits, enslaved plaintiffs usually had a far more difficult time accessing the evidence necessary to build a case. Whereas enslavers could rely on the contracts and mortgage agreements they themselves had created and registered with the state, enslaved plaintiffs often found themselves isolated and at a disadvantage, with neither the ability to create written evidence nor ready access to networks of individuals who could support their claims.

It was in these circumstances, where evidence was impossible to create and difficult to secure, that Betsey sued Pierre St. Amand for her freedom. In her failed attempt to prove what she knew to be true about herself and the past, we get a glimpse of the archival process of enslavement. This chapter is thus sometimes about Betsey and the development of a lawsuit, but it is mostly about how white men used paper, archives, jails, and courtrooms to transform Betsey into Rachel. It is a process that was uniquely, and only sometimes, visible in New Orleans's courtrooms. In this process, we find the extent of enslavers' archival power, which they could use to not only contradict an enslaved person's story about the past but also invalidate the history that entitled the enslaved person to freedom. In Betsey's experiences, we thus have an opportunity to learn about what the process of enslaving a free person looked like—a process that, by design, we cannot always see clearly.

When you read court records from a freedom suit, you are typically confronted with two stories: the first, an enslaver's, and the second, that of an enslaved person. Listening to and asking questions about both stories is important because each tells us something true and essential about the world as it then was: that enslavers' ability to create evidence of enslavement could be used to render a free person's past irrelevant. In Betsey's experiences, we thus find the terrible extent of enslavers' power. Telling her story cannot return her to freedom. It can, however, help us make sense of the circumstances that surrounded free people whom enslavers made disappear with contracts and archives, just as Betsey was supposed to.

Enslavement

On June 30, 1819, Betsey submitted a petition to the Orleans Parish Court wherein she identified herself as "Betsey otherwise called Rachel." The reasons why Betsey had to acknowledge that she was also "called Rachel" were at the center of her lawsuit. According to Betsey, she was "born free" in Cincinnati, Ohio, had lived "as a free person" in states including Ohio and Tennessee, and "never was sold or claimed as a slave until she was sold, first by one Erwin to Nathaniel Cannon and subsequently by Cannon to Pierre St. Amant," a resident of New Orleans, who now claimed Betsey as his enslaved property. Betsey, via her attorney William Orr, asked the court for three things: first, to order St. Amand to release her "from her illegal and unjust slavery"; second, to instruct St. Amand to "pay her all reasonable damages for her illegal detention"; and finally, to have the Orleans Parish Sheriff hire her out so that she could work for wages until the lawsuit was resolved.[3]

Throughout the antebellum period, enslaved people in Louisiana were not allowed to "be party in any civil action" save for instances when an enslaved individual had "claim to prove his freedom."[4] While I have yet to encounter a freedom suit in which an enslaved person suing for freedom testified on his or her own behalf, that is not to say that enslaved plaintiffs had nothing to say or offer in support of their claims. While Betsey's attorney surely wrote her petition, he would have had no idea what story to tell without Betsey's knowledge of her past. Petitions in these disputes were thus spaces for enslaved people, via their attorneys, to explain how they had become enslaved and to begin to demonstrate that they were entitled to their freedom. Of course, not every plaintiff told the same story.

In her August 1827 petition, Sarah Nicholson identified herself as a 24-year-old woman, born in Delaware to free parents. A year earlier, Nicholson's attorney explained, she was "stolen away from Pine Street wharf" in Philadelphia, taken aboard a brig, restrained with ropes, and taken southward to Louisiana, where she was sold as a slave.[5] In November 1835, Marian Tait sued the mayor, alderman, and inhabitants of the City of New Orleans for her freedom. Despite being born to free parents in South Carolina, Tait was arrested and imprisoned as a runaway slave.[6] When enslaved individuals argued that they were free, whether because of their place of birth or the contents of a will, the reasons for their enslavement remained much the same: as recognizably Black individuals, they were enslaved because it was possible for others to identify and treat them as slaves.

The petition that Betsey filed in June 1819 as well as the words of those who testified on her behalf provide some insight into her past and the circumstances surrounding her enslavement—or, rather, the version of the past that Betsey and her attorney believed would convince the court that she was entitled to her freedom. Betsey was born in Cincinnati, Ohio, likely in the late 1790s or early 1800s. Her mother was a free woman. They lived in Ohio when Betsey was a child, moving between Cincinnati and Mad River. Later, Betsey also spent time in Nashville, Tennessee, with her brother Bole, who owned a public house. In 1814, but possibly earlier, she worked as a cook on board barges as well as in several homes in Baton Rouge. During her travels, Betsey became acquainted with residents of Baton Rouge, New Orleans, and Natchez, Mississippi, some of whom would testify on her behalf, providing evidence that suggests Betsey was who she claimed to be.

On April 29, 1819, a white man by the name of Joseph Erwin filed a lawsuit that would change the course of Betsey's life. In his petition to the First Judicial District Court of Louisiana, Erwin via his attorney explained that he had previously sold John Hutchinson and Samuel Downey nine enslaved people—Patrick, Lawrence, Roger, Sam, Baptiste, Charles, Lizzy, Rachel, and Tabby—in Iberville Parish, Louisiana. Although Hutchinson and Downey had mortgaged these enslaved people to Erwin for the sum of $7,200, an outstanding debt of $800, which Hutchinson and Downey "neglected and refused to pay," remained. Additionally, Erwin noted, one of the enslaved people whom Hutchinson and Downey purchased, Rachel, was "now within the jurisdiction of this honorable court." While Erwin did not elaborate on Rachel or her location, he did request "an order of seizure . . . against the said slave Rachel and that she be sold by the Sheriff to satisfy the balance due." On May 6, 1819, Judge Joshua Lewis responded by instructing the Orleans Parish Sheriff to "seize and sell according to law, a colored negroe woman named Rachel."[7]

Rachel was not in John Hutchinson's or Samuel Downey's possession when Judge Lewis issued his order. Joseph Erwin told Cage—the man he hired to arrest Rachel—that he believed she was dead, and it is possible that she was. As all we have to learn about Rachel's life comes from contracts and mortgage agreements, documents that the men who created them swore described Betsey, we have no way of knowing where Rachel was when Cage arrested Betsey. It stands to reason, however, that Rachel was not in Hutchinson's or Downey's possession when Judge Lewis issued his order. To ensure he got his money back, Erwin identified Betsey as Rachel and hired Cage to arrest her "as a run away." There is no record of what this arrest looked like from Betsey's perspective; only Cage's remains. According to Cage, he approached Betsey in New Orleans's Faubourg St. Mary neighborhood, informing her that he was hired by Captain Erwin to "take her up as a runaway." She responded to the name Rachel, Cage claimed, explaining that she did not belong to Erwin but that he had sold her to Hutchinson and Downey, and she was now the property of someone named Mr. More who lived in the upper Faubourg. Cage then arrested Betsey and "lodged her in jail as a runaway" named Rachel.

I do not know how or why Joseph Erwin chose Betsey. In all likelihood, Betsey was also in the dark. As someone had previously stolen Betsey's freedom papers some years earlier, she was especially vulnerable, but I am unsure how and whether Erwin could have known this bit of information. Perhaps Erwin saw a stranger and took a chance? Maybe he thought Betsey looked like a traveler with no kin or community in close proximity who could help her demonstrate that she was free? Did he suspect she was a runaway herself? Whatever Erwin's reasons, he saw Betsey as someone whom he could claim as Rachel, and, to a large extent, he had the law on his side.

On June 7, 1806, the Territory of Orleans's legislature passed "an Act prescribing the rules and conduct to be observed with respect to Negroes and other Slaves of this territory," more commonly known as the Black Code, which remained in effect throughout the antebellum period. According to historian Judith Kelleher Schafer, the code's "main purpose" was the "regulation and control of the area's burgeoning slave population."[8] The code included specific regulations pertaining to the capture and exploitation of those deemed runaway slaves. According to section 32, if an enslaved person was found "absent from a house or dwelling, or where his usual place of working or residence is, without a white person accompanying him, and shall refuse to submit to the examination of any freeholder, the said freeholder shall be permitted to seize and correct the said slave." Section 27 provided free and enslaved people with a monetary incentive to arrest runaway enslaved people, stating that "the keeper of the jail of the county where a runaway may be caught, shall pay in cash or by giving his bond for every runaway slave delivered into his hands, to the person or persons, whether free or slave, who may have caught said runaway." According to section 28, those arrested and confined to the jail in New Orleans could be "directed by the sheriffs of the respective counties, to hard labor." During that time, the city council and sheriffs were supposed to "advertise said slaves at least in two newspapers of said city, in French and English," for three consecutive months, "and after that term once a month during the remainder of the year."

And if an enslaved person was not claimed within two years of the first published advertisement, reads section 29, it was the city treasurer's responsibility "to cause the said negroes to be sold." The proceeds of these sales, which took place at public auction, would then be used first to compensate the jailers and sheriffs who had imprisoned the enslaved person in question, and the remaining funds would be "deposited into the hands of the treasurer of the territory."[9]

Louisiana's laws thus outlined a process through which people of color were surveilled, arrested, and imprisoned as runaway slaves. Court records from other freedom suits demonstrate the pivotal role that arrests and local jails played in transforming free individuals into slaves. Of the 61 freedom suits tried before the Orleans Parish Court between 1813 and 1846, 32 include mentions of local New Orleans jails. Twenty-two of the plaintiffs in these 32 disputes describe being arrested, most as runaway slaves. Rachel, who sued for her freedom in the Orleans Parish Court in May 1820, explained in her petition that despite being "duly emancipated by a public act," a man by the name of Simon Knight "falsely and maliciously advertised your petitioner in the newspapers of this city as a runaway." Knight then brought Rachel to the jail "as his runaway slave and there as such forcibly and against her will detains and imprisons her although well knowing of her freedom."[10] In her 1834 petition to the Orleans Parish Court, Louisa Davis recounted how George Shall brought her "by force" to the police jail, where he "entered her on the books of said jail as her slave and ordered her to receive twenty five lashes, on a ladder which cruel treatment was accordingly instituted in the severest manner. And then the said George Shall," her petition continued, "ordered the jailor to put her in the streets to work with the chain negroes."[11]

When it came to enslaving free people of color, enslavers thus relied on their ability to identify and arrest individuals as runaway enslaved people. In the process, they created written records wherein they identified specific people as enslaved and sometimes assigned these imprisoned individuals different names. Peter, a free man of color, was arrested in September 1817 "under the name of Ben by a certain Mr. Haviland under a pretense that your petitioner was a slave of Mr. John Hutchins of Natchez."[12] Jean Baptiste Camille arrested Marie Joseph Meyon and "lodged [her] in the police jail of the Parish as his slave under the name of Lysida."[13] In his petition to the Orleans Parish Court, Mathias Gilbert recounted how he was detained by two persons who "charged him with being a runaway slave" and fixed "a false name upon him."[14] In assigning a free person a different name, enslavers continued the process of transforming free individuals into slaves, using jailkeepers' records to help them do so.

Arrests helped make Betsey's enslavement possible. Holland, a man working for Orleans Parish as either a jailer or a sheriff's deputy, testified that he recognized Betsey when she was brought to the jail, presumably by Cage. In 1816, just three years earlier, Betsey was arrested and imprisoned "as a free woman" on a charge of larceny. Though she was "discharged without prosecution," Holland explained, her time in jail yielded devastating effects. According to Mr. McFarland, another witness who may have also been employed by Orleans Parish, Betsey showed him her freedom papers while she was imprisoned as well as asked him to write a letter to someone whose name he could not recall. Later, Betsey accused some women who were imprisoned alongside her of stealing her freedom papers, raising such a disturbance that she was flogged into silence. Despite her best efforts to retrieve her papers, Betsey never got them back.[15] When Cage approached her and called her Rachel, she had no means of demonstrating that she was not Rachel. However, even if she had had her papers when Cage approached her, the same result was possible and even likely. Possession of one's freedom papers did not guarantee freedom. Still, losing her papers must have filled Betsey with terror, and I suspect that she may have hoped that whoever she was attempting to contact from jail might help her secure documentation of her status.

When Joseph Erwin ordered Cage to arrest and imprison Betsey as a runaway slave, he had not simply convinced Cage that Betsey was an enslaved woman named Rachel but had also effectively ensured that the state recognized her as such. By imprisoning Betsey, Erwin created a legitimate archival record of her status as enslaved property. He was able to do so, first, because Betsey was a woman of color, whom Erwin recognized and whom he knew others could recognize as a commodity, without a means of immediately demonstrating that she was a free woman; and second, because the law provided him with the power to imprison her as a slave. Betsey knew she was free when Cage approached and accused her of being an enslaved woman named Rachel, but what she knew about herself and her past was of no legal consequence. She did not possess and could not create any documentary evidence that could compel others to recognize her freedom, making her status, however rooted in reality, unverifiable. Betsey was a free woman in a place where others could identify her as a slave at their discretion and, by committing her to jail, could also create evidence of her status as enslaved property. By allowing residents to interrogate, seize, and arrest those they believed were runaway slaves, the state of Louisiana thus helped facilitate the enslavement of free people of color such as Betsey.

In the span of two weeks, Betsey was captured, imprisoned, and sold twice, making for a swift, terrifying transition from freedom to enslavement. On May 15, 1819, Holland delivered Betsey to Joseph Erwin. Then, three days later, on May 18, Erwin sold Betsey to Nathaniel R. Cannon, who then sold her to Pierre St. Amand. Any attempts she made to convince these men that she was Betsey, not Rachel, would likely have been met with threats and violent reprisals. Mathias Gilbert, who was also arrested as a runaway slave under a false name, would later describe the circumstances surrounding his arrest and subsequent sale in his petition to the Orleans Parish Court. As the unnamed men who captured and transported him to Baltimore tried to sell him, Gilbert repeatedly deterred many potential buyers from purchasing him "by his asserting that he was a freeman and relating to them his History." But asserting his freedom came at a heavy price. Gilbert was "cruelly and grievously punished" until, "intimidated by the severity of the punishment inflicted upon him and dreading a repetition of them," Gilbert thought it better "to be silent on the subject of his wrongs and in future not to deny that he was a slave."[16] Perhaps Betsey was also tortured or at the very least threatened into silence.

Somehow, likely from jail, Betsey was able to contact attorney William Orr and hire him to file a freedom suit on her behalf. To demonstrate that she was entitled to her freedom, Betsey would need to gather evidence and solicit testimony to tell a story she knew intimately well but could never prove on her own. In court, her freedom depended on her ability to present a well-evidenced historical narrative that was more compelling than her owner's, and she was at a tremendous disadvantage. Taking a closer look at the narratives that Betsey, Pierre St. Amand, and their respective attorneys worked to construct can help us make sense of how St. Amand was able to use written records to transform Betsey into Rachel.

The Plaintiff

In her petition to the Orleans Parish Court, Betsey claimed that she was entitled to her freedom because she was "born free" in Cincinnati, Ohio. To support her claim, Betsey and her attorney needed to construct a compelling historical narrative that began at the moment of her birth. Betsey was 1 of 20 plaintiffs in freedom suits tried before the Orleans Parish Court who claimed they were born free.[17] Records from 7 of these disputes do not include a verdict; they may have been dismissed at the time, but it is also possible that the pages that referenced the court's decision have since been misplaced. Of the remaining 13 freedom suits, plaintiffs in 7 cases successfully secured their freedom, and 6 cases were either dismissed or decided in favor of the defendant. By examining the cases these enslaved plaintiffs worked to build, we can begin to make sense of not only why Betsey was unable to convince the Orleans Parish Court that she was free but also the obstacles that enslaved individuals encountered when they sued for their freedom.

Betsey depended on eight people, seven white men and one white woman, to testify on her behalf. Each of these witnesses claimed they recognized her as a free woman of color named Betsey, not an enslaved woman named Rachel. Mrs. Winyard, whose first name was not included in court records, corroborated Betsey's claim that she had previously lived in Cincinnati. On March 24, 1820, Mrs. Winyard testified that she met Betsey, whom she had never known "by any other name than Betsey Johnson," 16 or 17 years earlier, in either 1803 or 1804. At the time, Betsey was four or five years of age and living in Cincinnati with her siblings and her mother who, according to Mrs. Winyard, "always passed as a free woman." Since then, Betsey and Mrs. Winyard had become reacquainted in New Orleans, where they lived "next door" to one another for at least two years leading up to Mrs. Winyard's testimony. Mrs. Winyard also testified that Betsey had a half sister by the name of Rachel who also passed as a free woman in New Orleans. But for all the information Mrs. Winyard was able to recall regarding Betsey, her family, and her life in Cincinnati and New Orleans, she was unable to corroborate Betsey's claims regarding her place of birth, testifying that she "doth not know that Betsey was born in Cincinnati" because Betsey was already four years old when they met.

Enslaved plaintiffs who claimed they were entitled to their freedom because of where and to whom they were born worked to gather the evidence and secure the testimony necessary to construct a historical narrative that began with their birth. Jesse Britain, who sued for his freedom in the Orleans Parish Court on September 14, 1818, claimed he was entitled to his freedom because he was born to a free woman of color in Fairfax County, Virginia. Britain did not offer any documentary evidence to support his claim, but he was able to secure two witnesses who were familiar with the circumstances surrounding his birth. On October 1, 1818, John Clain, a 23-year-old white man, testified on Britain's behalf. Clain stated that "he and plaintiff were born in [the] same neighborhood in Fairfax County Virginia, within half a mile of each other." He was also acquainted with Britain's mother, Venus, a "free woman [who] lived to herself and cultivated a piece of ground" and owned "cows and horses" in Virginia. Jesse Britain and John Clain remained friends and neighbors until Clain and his family moved to Kentucky, and they became reacquainted when living in New Orleans in 1817. David Williams, a free man of color, also testified on Britain's behalf. Williams claimed he "knew [the] plaintiff more than ten years ago in Fairfax County," where Britain attended school, receiving a "tolerable education." Williams was also acquainted with Jesse Britain's father, Ben Williams, and his mother, Venus, both of whom he "always knew" as free individuals.[18] On March 9, 1820, the Orleans Parish Court ruled in Jesse Britain's favor.

Whereas the two witnesses who testified on Jesse Britain's behalf were able to disclose specific details about Britain's parents that demonstrated they were free individuals—such as their ability to own property and send their child to school—Betsey was unable to locate any witnesses who possessed similar information about her past. Mrs. Winyard was not able to confirm that Betsey was born in Cincinnati, nor could she recall much information about Betsey's mother. But that is not to say that Betsey's claims about herself and her past were not rooted in reality. What Betsey was able to prove in court was a matter of what evidence she was able to secure and which individuals she was able to contact in a timely manner. Successfully reconstructing the past did not depend on a plaintiff's or defendant's accurate historical knowledge; it depended on who had the means to create and corroborate a historical narrative. While Jesse Britain had the good fortune of living in close proximity to two individuals who were both well acquainted with his history and willing to disclose it under oath, Betsey probably had no such network to fall back on. The outcome of these two lawsuits did not differ because Jesse Britain's narrative was more truthful than Betsey's; they differed because Betsey did not have access to evidence or a network of individuals who could and would verify her past.

Not unlike Mrs. Winyard, the remaining seven witnesses who testified on Betsey's behalf did not divulge any information about her place of birth. Their testimony does, however, provide us with a clearer picture of Betsey's life leading up to her arrest. Isaac Dorris, a white man who testified on March 24, 1820, claimed that he first became acquainted with Betsey 13 or 14 years earlier in Nashville, Tennessee, and had "never heard anything about the plaintiff's freedom nor did he ever hear she was claimed by any one as a slave." During his deposition, Dorris recalled that Betsey had a brother in Nashville by the name of Bole, who ran a "public house." He also happened to be acquainted with Joseph Erwin, who he did not believe "ever claimed the plaintiff as a slave." Dorris became reacquainted with Betsey in the previous three years while living in New Orleans, where "she passed" as a "free girl since he knew her to the best of his knowledge." When Dorris was asked whether he recognized the plaintiff as the same woman he described in his testimony, he answered that he believed she was "the same woman he knew at Nashville, and has no doubt of it at all."

William Davis, a white man and a planter who lived several miles south of Baton Rouge, Louisiana, also testified on Betsey's behalf. Davis first became acquainted with Betsey in either 1812 or 1813 in Natchez, Mississippi. He claimed that the plaintiff "went by the name of free Betsey" and that he had never heard she was "claimed by any one as a slave." Andrew Bird and William Bird, both of whom were deposed on Betsey's behalf in East Baton Rouge, Louisiana, claimed that they knew the plaintiff as a free woman of color with whom they had become acquainted in 1814. According to Andrew Bird, Betsey was not a slave; she was a free woman of color who worked on board a barge as a cook and who "passed as such in Baton Rouge without ever being interrupted on that account." William Bird confirmed that Betsey "was never molested by anybody" in regard to her freedom, which he acknowledged after "he made inquiries from several persons, who told him that she was free."

Isaac Dorris recognized Betsey as a free woman because of her reputation in Nashville and because he also recognized her brother Bole as a free man. William Davis decided that Betsey was a free woman when he heard others call her by the name "free Betsey." Andrew Bird determined that Betsey was a free woman because he never witnessed another person accuse Betsey of being a slave. William Bird determined that Betsey was free only after making "inquiries from several persons, who told him that she was free." None of the aforementioned witnesses testified that they ever asked Betsey whether she was free or enslaved or that they requested that she show them her freedom papers, suggesting that Betsey's status as a free woman depended on the recognition of others in most every space and not always on written evidence—that is, until it did. Betsey relied on others' willingness to distinguish between a woman of color who was enslaved and a woman of color who was free. And it was men such as Isaac Dorris and William Davis who made decisions about what was acceptable evidence of Betsey's freedom, not Betsey. Here lies the root of the tenuous circumstances of Betsey's freedom: that it was potentially subject to scrutiny at every moment and that it could always require different, unpredictable standards of verification. Even beyond the space of a courtroom and the context of a freedom suit, Betsey could discover that her knowledge of her past and the reasons she was entitled to her freedom were painfully insufficient evidence of her status as a free woman.

The Defendant

As a defendant in a freedom suit, Pierre St. Amand was interested in protecting his investment in the plaintiff, regardless of the court's decision. He did not need to personally have much information about Rachel's or Betsey's past in order to do so, as he was able to rely on the state to gather the documentary evidence and secure the witnesses necessary to build his case. St. Amand submitted four documents to the Orleans Parish Court as evidence. Document A was a certificate of mortgages, Document B was a notarial contract wherein the parties involved in a mortgage agreed to dissolve it, Document C was a private bill of sale, and Document D was a notarial contract. St. Amand himself neither possessed any of the documentary evidence he submitted nor was previously acquainted with any of the witnesses who testified on his behalf. The evidence and networks he relied on to create the history of transactions and mortgages necessary to make Betsey into Rachel were created and maintained by enslavers in conjunction with the state of Louisiana. Examining the case that Pierre St. Amand and his allies built and considering how he was able to build it reveal how defendants in freedom suits could rely on their privileged relationship with the state not only to build cases during freedom suits but also to avoid losing their investments regardless of a court's decision.

On March 27, 1820, Pierre St. Amand submitted a copy of a notarial contract that included the terms of his purchase of an enslaved woman named Rachel from Nathaniel R. Cannon. The contract, which he and Cannon signed before New Orleans notary Phillippe Pendesclaux on May 22, 1819, was one that the state of Louisiana had acknowledged and archived. St. Amand was thus able to rely on the state to secure evidence that proved not only that he had purchased the plaintiff as an enslaved woman but also that the state had recognized her as a person who could be sold. The contract also established that Nathaniel R. Cannon had sold the plaintiff to St. Amand, which allowed St. Amand to call Cannon into court as a defendant to effectively support his claim to Rachel.

Because slave buyers and sellers in Louisiana were supposed to document their transactions in writing and register their contracts with the state, plaintiffs and defendants involved in civil suits concerning enslaved people could often rely on the state when it came to gathering the documentary evidence necessary to support their claims. When Pierre St. Amand responded to Betsey's lawsuit, he did not submit the original contract that he and Nathaniel R. Cannon signed before New Orleans notary Philippe Pendesclaux. Instead, he had Pendesclaux transcribe and submit a copy of the contract to the Orleans Parish Court. Below the transcription, Pendesclaux wrote the following: "I do hereby certify the above to be a true copy of the original on Record in my office in witness whereof I have hereunto set my hand and seal." Because St. Amand purchased Betsey using an authentic act of sale, he could rely on the state's archive to secure evidence when his right to possess his newly acquired enslaved property was challenged. The authentic act of sale was proof of the obligations between St. Amand and Cannon, and in the context of a freedom suit, St. Amand could use it as evidence to demonstrate that both he and the state had recognized the plaintiff as a person who could be sold and owned.

The contract that Pierre St. Amand used to purchase Betsey was also evidence that he could use to transform Nathaniel Cannon into a defendant. It was in Cannon's interest to disclose information, seek out evidence, and locate witnesses who would allow St. Amand to maintain possession of the plaintiff, if only to avoid having to reimburse St. Amand himself. Indeed, the fact that St. Amand and Cannon appeared in court to respond to Betsey's lawsuit on the same day and with the same attorney, G. Wikoff, suggests that their interests were very much aligned. In addition to submitting a copy of the notarial contract as evidence, the defense also presented several documents relating to a sale and mortgage agreement between Joseph Erwin, John Hutchinson, and Samuel Downey. Once more, St. Amand and Cannon were able to secure these documents because the state of Louisiana preserved them.

Louisiana's 1808 Civil Code defined a mortgage as "a contract by which a person affects the whole of his property or only some part of it, in favor of another, for security of an engagement, but without divesting himself of the possession thereof."[19] The 1825 Civil Code refined the definition, but in spirit it remained much the same.[20] Mortgages were further divided into conventional, legal, and judicial mortgages.[21] Conventional mortgages reflected an agreement between several parties; judicial mortgages were the result of a court's judgment; and a legal mortgage was an agreement created by the law alone.[22] Throughout the antebellum period, conventional mortgages were valid only if they were documented under private signature or in an authentic act.[23] Thus, when John Hutchinson and Samuel Downey mortgaged nine enslaved people, including Rachel, to Joseph Erwin for $7,200 on February 2, 1813, they were supposed to put the terms of their agreement in writing, either privately or before a Louisiana notary.

Although parties who entered into a conventional mortgage were allowed to record their agreement in a private act, they were also supposed to register their agreement with the state in order for the obligations outlined therein to be valid against a third party.[24] The 1808 Civil Code required consenting parties to register conventional mortgages in New Orleans in a "public *folio* book kept for that purpose in the city of New-Orleans for the whole territory."[25] As of 1825, parties were (on paper) allowed to register their agreements with parish judges outside of New Orleans, but the city still maintained the office of the recorder of mortgages, who was responsible for maintaining several registers, including one that contained "all acts from which there results a conventional or legal mortgage, or privilege."[26] Throughout the antebellum period, these officers were bound to deliver a "certificate of the mortgages" to any individual who requested information regarding a specific piece of property, including enslaved property.[27]

On February 2, 1813, Joseph Erwin, John Hutchinson, and Samuel Downey appeared before Iberville Parish judge John Dutton. Dutton and Downey purchased and agreed to mortgage nine enslaved people to Erwin for $7,200. Seven years later, Pierre St. Amand's and Nathaniel R. Cannon's attorney, G. Wikoff, requested and received a certificate of mortgages from New Orleans's recorder of mortgages, a document he subsequently presented as evidence to the Orleans Parish Court. The certificate, dated March 18, 1820, confirmed that Hutchinson and Downey had mortgaged nine enslaved people, including an enslaved woman named Rachel, "in favor of" Erwin "to secure the payment of seven thousand two hundred Dollars."[28] By obtaining the certificate, Wikoff effectively bolstered Pierre St. Amand and Nathaniel Cannon's claims that the plaintiff was an enslaved woman named Rachel.

St. Amand also submitted a private bill of sale as evidence. The contract was penned by Joseph Erwin, and it bore Erwin's signature as well as the signature of N. Wilson, a person who witnessed the transaction. It stated that on May 18, 1819, Erwin "sold and delivered" a "negro woman named Rachel" to Nathaniel Cannon for $800. Once again, this was not a document that St. Amand had in his possession; in all likelihood, it was Cannon who provided the aforementioned document, as it confirmed that he had purchased an enslaved woman named Rachel from Joseph Erwin. Three days after Betsey filed her lawsuit in the Orleans Parish Court, St. Amand and his attorney, G. Wikoff, submitted their response to the court. St. Amand maintained that he was the "true and legal owner of the negress Betsey alias Rachel," who he accused of claiming "the right of freedom without any maintainable ground or reason." He then asked the court to instruct Nathaniel R. Cannon to appear in order to "guarantee your respondent against all damages which he may sustain in this suit and to confirm his right titles in said negress." Paper made it possible for St. Amand to gain an ally in his endeavor to demonstrate that the plaintiff was a slave named Rachel.

St. Amand's request that Cannon appear in court was similar to a defendant in a slave-centered redhibition suit asking that a previous owner be called to court as a means of avoiding being held liable if the court issued a verdict in favor of the plaintiff. By calling on Cannon, St. Amand had effectively ensured that his investment in Betsey was secure regardless of the Orleans Parish Court's decision. For instance, when Sarah Nicholson sued Edward Livingston Thompson for her freedom in the Orleans Parish Court in August 1827, Livingston responded by requesting that Pressley Stephenson, from whom he purchased Nicholson, "be cited in warranty according to law to come in and defend this suit." He also asked that if the plaintiff "should succeed in obtaining her freedom, the said Stephenson shall be decreed to pay your respondent back the amount of purchase," approximately $325. When the Orleans Parish Court ruled in Sarah Nicholson's favor, the judge included the following in his written decision: "And whereas the said Defendant did call in warrantee this vendor Pressley Stephenson as per authentic deed of sale annexed to his answer, it is further ordered and decreed that the Defendant shall have his recourse against him for the reimbursement of the price being 325 dollars together with the amount of costs and compensations allowed as aforesaid by the court."[29] For enslavers, acts of sale were thus sometimes worth producing, if only to ensure that one's investment remained as secure as possible.

Joseph Thompson, Abraham Wright, Samuel M. Spraggins, and Cage each testified on behalf of the defendant in *Betsey alias Rachel v. St. Amand* (1819). Thompson and Wright were in Joseph Erwin's employ as early as 1806 and 1807, and Wright and Spraggins were in the slave trading and real estate business with Erwin. Alice Pemble White, whose master's thesis centered the experiences of Joseph Erwin and his wife, Lavinia Erwin, in Louisiana, described Abraham Wright as "Erwin's loyal and trusted agent."[30] And Cage was working for Erwin when he arrested Betsey in May 1819. The notarial contract that Pierre St. Amand and Nathaniel Cannon signed on May 22, 1819, contained no mention of Joseph Erwin, and if Cannon had been inclined to withhold information about his purchase from St. Amand, it would have proven difficult for St. Amand to locate any of these witnesses, because he would have had no idea where to look. But because Cannon was invested in the outcome of the lawsuit, if only to avoid having to reimburse St. Amand, Cannon was likely able to contact the aforementioned witnesses through Joseph Erwin.

Each of these witnesses was essential to Pierre St. Amand's and Nathaniel Cannon's defense. Of the four who testified on St. Amand's behalf, only Cage was deposed in the presence of the plaintiff and defendant. Samuel Spraggins was deposed before a justice of the peace in New Orleans, and Joseph Thompson and Abraham Wright testified before a justice of the peace in Iberville Parish. Each of them claimed that they believed that the plaintiff was Rachel, an enslaved woman or, in Cage's case, that he recognized the plaintiff in court as Rachel. While a defendant's ability to present written evidence mattered, it was not always, in itself, sufficient proof that a plaintiff should be enslaved. In addition to documentary evidence that proved that the plaintiff had been treated as a slave, defendants in freedom suits depended on witnesses to confirm that the person described in the contents of a contract or a mortgage certificate was the plaintiff.

For instance, on July 14, 1831, Venus Davenport filed a freedom suit in the Orleans Parish Court. In her petition, Venus explained that she was previously enslaved but was freed when John Stanley, her owner, took her to Illinois, where slavery "was prohibited by law." She claimed that she "became free" because for at least 21 years, she resided in Illinois with Stanley's "knowledge and consent." Since then, Samuel D. Dixon had claimed Venus as his enslaved property. Although Dixon denied Davenport's claims and submitted a private act of sale as evidence, he was unable to convince the Orleans Parish Court that Davenport was his slave. While Davenport was unable to secure any documentary evidence, several individuals who testified on her behalf confirmed that she was in Illinois, with her owner's consent, when the state adopted its constitution, which outlawed slavery and would have effectively rendered her free. In his written decision, Judge Charles Maurian explained that even if Dixon's act of sale did "bear upon the face of it any mark of authenticity or genuineness, which in the opinion of this court it does not, still it would not of itself be sufficient evidence of the Defendant's right to hold the plaintiff in slavery."[31] There were thus moments when judges could and did interrogate the validity of a bill of sale. Paper mattered, but it was not always all-powerful.

Each of the witnesses who testified on behalf of Pierre St. Amand helped connect the plaintiff to the documentary evidence that St. Amand and Nathaniel Cannon submitted to the Orleans Parish Court. When

Abraham Wright and Joseph Thompson testified on September 9, 1819, they confirmed that they believed the plaintiff was the same woman Joseph Erwin purchased from "two men, brothers by the name of Smith" in North Carolina in 1806 and 1807 and trafficked to Louisiana by way of Tennessee. Samuel Spraggins testified that he met Rachel in either 1806 or 1807 on Joseph Erwin's plantation in Iberville Parish, Louisiana. He confirmed that Erwin attempted to sell Rachel twice, but she "reverted two distinct times" to Erwin because the buyers were "incapable of fulfilling their engagements but not on account of the purchasers having any objection as to the title." Ultimately, Spraggins claimed, Erwin was finally able to sell Rachel to Nathaniel Cannon, who then sold her to Pierre St. Amand. Cage, who was deposed before the Orleans Parish Court on March 27, 1820, described how he arrested the plaintiff, "whom he now recognizes in court." By testifying that he knew the plaintiff was Rachel, Cage was able to bolster Joseph Thompson's, Abraham Wright's, and Samuel Spraggins's respective claims that the plaintiff was an enslaved woman named Rachel who was previously Joseph Erwin's property.

Erwin's, Wright's, and Spraggins's testimony effectively connected the plaintiff to the documents that Pierre St. Amand and Nathaniel Cannon submitted to the court as evidence. And because Cage was able to confirm that Erwin recognized the plaintiff as his enslaved property less than two months earlier, his testimony helped bridge the gap between an 1813 mortgage and an 1819 act of sale. While none of the aforementioned witnesses was acquainted with St. Amand, they were nevertheless instrumental in helping him construct his history of Rachel. St. Amand's personal knowledge, or lack thereof, regarding the plaintiff's history was of no consequence, because as a defendant in a freedom suit, he was able to rely on the state to collect written evidence, to access a network of buyers and sellers who were invested in supporting his claims, and to ensure that his investment in the plaintiff was secure, regardless of the outcome of the lawsuit. It should be noted, however, that none of the documents that Pierre St. Amand and Nathaniel R. Cannon submitted as evidence proved that the plaintiff was Rachel. At best, they demonstrated that an enslaved woman whom enslavers agreed to call Rachel had been sold several times between 1813 and 1819. Nevertheless, it was evidence that St. Amand and Cannon were ultimately able to use to convince the Orleans Parish Court and, during a subsequent appeal, the Louisiana Supreme Court that the plaintiff was an enslaved woman named Rachel.

In his lengthy written decision, Orleans Parish Judge James Pitot described *Betsey, alias Rachel, f.w.c. v. St. Amand* (1819) as an "intricate and troubling case." What seems to have disturbed Pitot most was that the case depended "on one side, upon mere testimony which far from being constantly both positive and concordant, is besides, wholly unsupported by any written document whatsoever." The judge conceded that while "some doubts might surely have been entertained" regarding the identity of the plaintiff, she ultimately "did not establish her pretended right to liberty." On April 25, 1820, Judge Pitot issued a verdict in favor of the defendant. The Louisiana Supreme Court would reaffirm the lower court's decision in June of that year.

Pierre St. Amand did not need to look too far beyond the written record to convince the Orleans Parish Court and the Louisiana Supreme Court that Betsey was Rachel. The legal obligations between slave buyers and sellers in Louisiana, as well as state-archived contracts and mortgage agreements, provided St. Amand with a means of accessing all the evidence and witnesses he needed to convince the Orleans Parish Court that the plaintiff was his enslaved property. He did not have to possess extensive knowledge regarding Rachel's or Betsey's respective histories to do so, nor did he need to prove that the plaintiff had been legally enslaved—for instance, by securing witnesses who could confirm that she was born to an enslaved woman. Histories of sales and mortgages, created and tied together by enslavers, were more than sufficient. The archive and the courtroom favored enslavers.

Enslavers' relationships with the state were such that they could create and gather evidence that made specific individuals recognizable as enslaved property. As a free woman of color, Betsey enjoyed no such privileges. The depositions of those who testified on Betsey's behalf reveal that even beyond the space of the courtroom, her status as a free woman was dependent on the recognition of others, was always potentially subject to question, and could, at any moment, require verification with evidence that she could not always provide. Pierre St. Amand knew little to nothing about Betsey's or Rachel's history, but he was still able to make Betsey recognizable as his enslaved property in court because he had the means to create and access the evidence and to secure the witnesses necessary to corroborate his version of her past.

Not every enslaver used an act of sale to enslave someone they knew to be free, but they could have. And if they had, the vast majority of those enslaved, their lives and their pasts, remain unrecognizable to us now. Only court records from freedom suits render the processes of commodification that ensnared people such as Betsey visible. This is no accident. Enslaved people bought and sold in New Orleans were supposed to be historicized only in specific ways—namely, in terms of relationships between buyers and sellers, creditors and debtors. Contracts were spaces where enslavers could and did erase an individual's history in favor of depicting a person as an interchangeable commodity, which is why Pierre St. Amand was able to enslave Betsey without knowing anything about her past and without demonstrating the origins of her enslavement. It was enslavers' unique archival relationship with the state made Betsey's transformation into Rachel possible.

CHAPTER 5

Sarah Ann Connor

Freedom and the Archive

How does one tell the story of an elusive emancipation
and a travestied freedom? Certainly, reconsidering the
meaning of freedom entails looking critically at the
production of historical narratives since the very effort to
represent the situation of the subaltern reveals the provi-
sionality of the archive as well as the interests that shape it
and thereby determine the emplotment of history.

—SAIDIYA HARTMAN, *Scenes of Subjection*

ON APRIL 11, 1846, Sarah Ann Connor sued Theophilus Freeman for her
freedom. In her petition, Connor alleged that some five years earlier, in
July 1841, Jane Shelton—a white woman who had claimed Connor as
her enslaved property since 1838—sold Connor to Theophilus Freeman
for $700 of Connor's money and for the purposes of releasing her from
slavery. Since then, Sarah Connor claimed, "she had been in the actual
enjoyment of her freedom undisturbed by the said Freeman or any other
person." The only reason she was filing suit, she explained via her attorney, was because "Freeman has become embarrassed and unable to pay
his debts"; as a result, Connor was concerned that one of his creditors
might mistake her for Freeman's enslaved property. She thus sued him
to ensure that her freedom was "beyond all doubt or question secured
to her" as well as to create "some public evidence upon the records of the
country that she is a free woman." Unlike plaintiffs in other freedom
suits, Sarah Connor did not ask the court to order Theophilus Freeman
to free her, because he already had; instead, she asked the state to produce

evidence that would compel others, especially Freeman's creditors, to see her as she had seen herself since 1841: as a free woman.[1]

Connor, f.w.c. v. Freeman (1846) marked the first time Sarah Connor used the courts to protect her freedom, but it would not be the last. When Mary Ann and Ellen, two enslaved women, were repossessed to compensate for Theophilus Freeman's debts, Connor sued Freeman's creditors, claiming that she was Mary Ann and Ellen's "true and lawful owner," not Freeman.[2] Freeman's creditors, in turn, responded with accusations of their own, namely, that Sarah Connor was Theophilus Freeman's slave, concubine, and means of concealing his assets from his creditors.

In the process of fighting to gain possession of Mary Ann and Ellen, Sarah Ann Connor lost her freedom, at least for a while. While the Louisiana Supreme Court would eventually overturn the decision that returned her to enslavement, the fact that Connor's freedom was so easily won and lost tells us that the stakes involved in participating in the business of slavery depended on an enslaver's race and gender. For women like Connor, it was the possibility of enslavement that shaped and constrained their ability to exercise the privileges of their legal freedom, privileges that included enslaving others.

Sarah Connor was never denied access to New Orleans courtrooms, but when she filed lawsuits to protect her investments in the people she claimed as her enslaved property, opposing attorneys questioned her status as a free woman and her ability to act independently of a man who did not own her, forcing Connor to fight a battle on multiple fronts. Instead of simply providing contracts to support her claims in a common property dispute, she was forced, time and time again, to defend her freedom. On paper and according to the letter of the law, Connor was able to sign affidavits, create acts of sale, register notarial contracts, and file civil suits—engaging in the archival production necessary to effectively participate in the business of slavery—but in reality, using the privileges of her freedom had consequences that, while not codified, were nevertheless real and extremely dangerous. To determine what Connor's lived experiences can tell us about the business of slavery and the world as it then was, we must consider what the law said Sarah Connor could do as a free woman alongside how her race, gender, relationship, and previous status as an enslaved woman shaped and constrained her choices as an enslaver, plaintiff, and defendant.

This chapter is about how and why Sarah Ann Connor lost her freedom. Because most every piece of direct evidence we have to learn about Connor from this period comes from court records and contracts, learning about Connor herself—not the Sarah Connor she needed to be to defend her freedom or the "notorious Sarah Connor,"[3] as her enemies tried to depict her—is difficult. Still, there is room to draw some informed conclusions about her, especially in regard to how she understood her freedom and the possibilities it entailed. Connor's actions, at least those we can see from when and where we are now, tell us something about what she could do in the world as it then was, but only if we do the work necessary to distinguish "between what happened and that which was said to have happened," what Michel-Rolph Trouillot calls historicity 1 and historicity 2.[4]

You can tell a lot of stories about Sarah Ann Connor. It was true during her lifetime, and it remains true today. I am not the first historian to write about her. She briefly appears in Judith K. Schafer's *Slavery, the Civil Law, and the Supreme Court of Louisiana* as well as in Walter Johnson's *Soul by Soul*.[5] Connor is also the subject of a chapter in Alexandra J. Finley's *An Intimate Economy*. Whereas Schaffer and Johnson use Connor as an example on the road to drawing conclusions about white male enslavers, Finley "sifts through the myriad portrayals of Conner to see what of her survives the violence of the archive." In closely examining Connor's life in New Orleans, Finley demonstrates that for Connor, "the sexual economy of slavery meant that even as a free woman of color, her right to own her body was never secure."[6] Like Finley, I am interested in what we can learn about Sarah Connor from the written archive. Specifically, I want to understand what was at stake when she acted as an enslaver. In a business in which archival production was an important part of exploiting one's enslaved property, where did and could Sarah Connor fit in? And what were the possibilities and limits that shaped her choices and their consequences? The answers to these questions stand to teach us something important about the nature of enslavers' archival power: that it was defined not only by a person's ability to write things down, access notaries, and enter spaces such as courtrooms but also by one's race and gender.

Sarah and the Law

By 1838, Sarah Ann Connor was the property of Jane Shelton, a white woman who resided in New Orleans. Shelton allowed Connor to hire herself out and live separately in the city. It is possible that in these circumstances, Connor started learning about Louisiana law and what she could do with it. Someone or something in the world she lived in taught Connor that self-purchase was an avenue to freedom. Whatever her source or sources of information, her perception was indeed in line with Article 174 of Louisiana's Civil Code, which stated, "The slave is incapable of making any contract, except those which relate to his own emancipation."[7] Of course, she may have also known that the path to such arrangements could be rocky and uncertain. Judith K. Schafer's work tells us that negotiations between enslaved people and their enslavers in antebellum Louisiana were usually informal and not in writing, leaving enslaved people vulnerable to enslavers' changing minds and whims. No matter how much money an enslaved person managed to accumulate, it was ultimately up to an owner to decide whether to accept the terms of a self-purchase. I wonder how and when Sarah Connor started saving her money. Did she ask Jane Shelton if she would consider a sale? Did Shelton give her blessing and name her price? Or did Connor simply begin saving, hoping she could talk Shelton into a deal when the time came?[8]

Between 1838 and 1841, Connor lived and worked out of a New Orleans boardinghouse on Burgundy Street, washing clothes and renting out rooms, passing on a portion of her wages to Shelton and saving what she could for herself. When a man who was staying at the boardinghouse asked her why she "worked so hard," Connor replied, "she was a slave desirous of earning her freedom."[9] According to the testimony of Melissa Garrison, a free woman of color who probably counted herself among Connor's friends, there was a "griffe woman" who "kept Connor's money for her" in a "mahogany box."[10] This suggests at least two things: first, Connor had people in her community whom she trusted; and second, Connor did not trust Jane Shelton enough to store her money with her. This, of course, does not necessarily mean that Shelton was opposed to selling Connor, to herself or anyone else. However, Theophilus Freeman's involvement in the sale implies that Shelton may not have been willing to engage with Connor alone. If she had been, why involve Freeman at all?

Theophilus Freeman was a slave trader. In *Twelve Years a Slave*, Solomon Northup describes him as "a tall, thin-faced man, with light complexion and a little bent."[11] Enslaved people like Northup, whom Freeman worked to sell, knew he could be cruel and violent. But what did Sarah Connor know? How did she see Freeman? How did she believe he saw her? These were questions that someone desirous of their freedom, someone intent on using Freeman to achieve her own ends, may have asked herself and, possibly, others. She likely involved him in her self-purchase because she had to and because she trusted him or, at the very least, hoped she could trust him. Because we can only glimpse the transaction through contracts and court records, it is difficult to know much about the beginnings of their relationship and what transpired when; the story changed depending on who was doing the telling.

According to Sarah Connor and Theophilus Freeman—at least when they were before a New Orleans court—Freeman bought Connor from Jane Shelton with Connor's money in order to release her from slavery. When Connor sued Freeman for her freedom, she and her attorney presented two pieces of evidence, both dated July 12, 1841, to support this particular claim: the first, a copy of the notarial contract Shelton and Freeman signed when Shelton sold Connor to Freeman; the second, a private act of sale that described Freeman selling Connor to herself. Each of these documents bore Jane Shelton's signature, although Shelton remembered signing the second years after the first. She also told different stories about what her intentions were when she made the sale. When she testified in *Dunbar v. Connor, f.w.c.* (1849)—a lawsuit Alden F. Dunbar filed against Connor on behalf of Freeman's creditors—Shelton claimed that she sold Connor "to be free."[12] But when she testified in Connor's lawsuit against the Bank of Kentucky, Shelton claimed that when she sold Connor to Freeman, she "did not stipulate that Connor should be free nor did she care anything about it." All she "intended to do at the time of the sale" was expressed in the notarial contract she and Freeman signed.[13] Theophilus's creditors would use Jane Shelton's testimony to argue that Sarah Connor and Theophilus Freeman had backdated the private act of sale to fraudulently secure Connor's freedom, but that's another story.

Regardless of Jane Shelton's intentions or when the private act of sale was created, Theophilus Freeman and Sarah Connor participated in the July 1841 sale in order to secure Connor's freedom. We know this because after the sale, Connor and Freeman traveled together for the purposes of solidifying Connor's freedom; and we know that Connor believed she was free when she returned to New Orleans from states where slavery was illegal because she lived like a free woman, purchasing enslaved people and running her own business. It is thus likely that Sarah Connor believed her status was firmly in place right up until the moment when Theophilus Freeman's creditors came calling.[14]

William H. Williams filed a lawsuit against Theophilus Freeman in the Orleans Parish Court. In his petition, via his attorney, Williams claimed that Freeman owed him $15,890.56 and asked the court to order Freeman to pay him. To prove that the debt existed, Williams presented a private promissory note dated July 5, 1842, meaning that the note had not been documented or archived by a notary or other state official. And as Freeman conceded that the note was indeed legitimate, the court decided in Williams's favor on March 31, 1843. Then, Williams transferred the judgment to Junius Amis, meaning Freeman now owed the $15,890.56 to Amis. To ensure that Freeman fulfilled his obligation, the court began ordering members of the Orleans Parish sheriff's department to seize his property. On July 7, 1843, Deputy Sheriff H. Tobin repossessed four enslaved people named Bob, Peggy, Sam, and Sarah; on June 29, 1844, Sarah, Elizabeth, and Elizabeth's two-year-old child were seized; and finally, on December 12, 1844, Sarah and Robert were repossessed.

This is where things get complicated. In May 1844, more than a year after the court made its decision, attorneys for Oliver D. Grant and William Barton, partners in a New York firm, filed a motion wherein they argued that the proceedings in *Williams v. Freeman* (1843) were "simulated and fraudulent." According to Grant and Barton, they had previously won a lawsuit against Freeman and were entitled to the property that had been seized thus far. Additionally, they claimed, "the judgment conferred by said Freeman in favor of the Plaintiff Williams was simulated and fraudulent and made without consideration and the transfer of the same to Junius Amis was of the said character, and the ownership and control of the said Judgment is in the said Freeman." In short, Oliver Grant and William Barton accused Freeman, Williams, and Amis of orchestrating a lawsuit so that they could have a court-sponsored means of moving Freeman's money around without it ever leaving Freeman's control.[15]

At the time, Sarah Connor and Freeman were living together at 163 Gravier Street. She was furnishing and renting out rooms, including a space to Freeman just outside the home, which he used as his slave yard. According to records from *Williams v. Freeman* (1843), members of the Orleans Parish sheriff's department seized 13 enslaved people to compensate for Freeman's outstanding debt. Three of these individuals were named Sarah, at least according to the men who did the seizing. And if we believe Samuel Powers, an Orleans Parish sheriff's deputy, Sarah Connor was one of them.

If Connor was forcibly taken from her home, it would have been in either July 1843 or June 1844. While her arrest was temporary, she would have had no way of knowing that at the time, and she must have been terrified. She was not the only person in that home who experienced terror; those seized alongside her probably felt it, too. As an enslaver, Connor was more than capable of inspiring terror herself, likely using threats, coercion, and violence to wield authority over the enslaved, domestically and elsewhere.[16] Enslaved individuals taken alongside Connor, those who witnessed her seizure from a safe distance, and those who learned about these events later may have experienced fear for themselves as well as their friends and loved ones, perhaps mixed with some sense of satisfaction in watching the Orleans Parish sheriff's deputies take Connor. Her seizure would have reminded all that Sarah Connor was at once an enslaver and enslavable.[17]

When Samuel Powers helped his colleagues seize Connor, he may have knocked at the door of the boardinghouse where Connor and Freeman lived and worked. He could have handed whoever answered the door a written notice that justified their presence and what happened next. He may have given additional explanations, but he just as easily could have offered none at all. He was a sheriff's deputy, and his commission depended on arresting whomever he could find and identify as Theophilus Freeman's property. Powers was motivated and powerful, and Sarah Connor was a woman of color in her home. She was vulnerable. She may have protested, offering explanations not so far removed from the evidence she would provide when she sued Theophilus for her freedom in 1846, but whatever she said or did fell on deaf ears. Connor could own enslaved people, run a thriving business, and travel freely to states where slavery was outlawed, but in that moment, faced with a real, horrifying challenge to her status, she had nothing and could do nothing to compel Powers to acknowledge her freedom's existence.

After removing Sarah Connor and at least one other enslaved person from the home, Samuel Powers and his colleagues probably took them to the Orleans Parish prison, where he was the chief warden.[18] Some time afterward—though I am not sure how long it would have taken or even whether Theophilus Freeman may have already known—the slave trader learned that several enslaved people had been taken from his home. He offered a bond in order to take possession of Connor; I do not know whether he did the same for those seized alongside her. Although I know that Connor was able to return home, at the moment of seizure I lose any discernible archival trace of most of the individuals who were taken to compensate for Freeman's debts. And if Freeman had not worked to bring Connor home, I might have lost her here, too.

Sarah Connor's sense of fear and dread may have waned when she returned to 163 Gravier, but it would not have entirely dissipated. This was not over. She knew it, and so did Freeman. Sheriff's deputies kept coming to the house to take human beings until at least 1851, and I suspect any knock at the door would have caused Connor's heart to race. Most everything Connor did next was indicative of her sincere desire to ensure that she could never again be mistaken for Theophilus Freeman's enslaved property.

Before Connor ever set foot in a courtroom, she probably learned that her previous status and her ongoing relationship with Freeman made her vulnerable. She then made a decision to use what she knew about the law and the courts to sue Freeman for her freedom, and she won. In that moment, verdict in hand, recognized by the state as a free woman, Connor may have believed she was safe or, at the very least, safer than she was before. According to Louisiana's Civil Code, "an emancipation once perfected is irrevocable."[19] But arrests and freedom suits tried in Orleans Parish tell us that was not always the case. At the very least, Connor felt secure enough in her status to venture into court to protect her enslaved property, to make use of the rights and privileges that men like Bernard Kendig and Theophilus Freeman probably took for granted.

The Plaintiff

In April 1848, Orleans Parish Sheriff Joe Lewis repossessed four enslaved people—Mary Ann, Ellen, Isam, and Emmanuel—to compensate for Theophilus Freeman's debts.[20] Almost immediately, injunctions and lawsuits to prevent their sale were filed—not by Theophilus, but by Sarah Connor and Junius Amis. Connor and Amis filed separate lawsuits, with the same attorneys, against Freeman's creditors, including the Bank of Kentucky and Alden F. Dunbar, who was then acting as a representative on behalf of Freeman's creditors.[21] In her petition, Connor claimed that she was the "true and lawful owner" of Mary Ann and Ellen. Junius made the same argument about Isam and Emmanuel in his petition.[22] Lawyers representing the Bank of Kentucky and Alden Dunbar responded to Amis and Connor's respective lawsuits with accusations of fraud, yet the differences between these accusations are important: whenever Amis was accused of working to defraud Freeman's creditors, his legal standing as a free person was never called into question.

By 1850, Junius Amis was a resident of Madison Parish, Louisiana, who owned 164 enslaved people. According to that year's census, Amis was a North Carolina–born planter whose real estate was valued at $70,000. In May 1848, he filed two lawsuits: the first, against Alden F. Dunbar, and the second, against the Bank of Kentucky. The petitions in the two lawsuits mirrored each other. According to Amis, he was "the true and lawful owner" of two enslaved men, Emmanuel and Isam, and he had been "in the peaceable, sole, and undisturbed possession" of them until April 1848, when Orleans Parish sheriff John L. Lewis repossessed them to compensate for Freeman's debts. Amis thus asked that Emmanuel and Isam be returned to his possession. Robert R. Mott, a lawyer representing the Bank of Kentucky, claimed that Amis's allegations were "untrue." He explained that Freeman was insolvent and had "for many years past" used Amis's name "as a cover and shield to his own transactions for the purposes of hiding and concealing his property from the pursuit of his [Freeman's] creditors." In reality, Mott continued, Amis never had any title to Isam and Emmanuel, and if he did have such a title, it was "simulated," "void," and made for the purposes of "defrauding" Freeman's creditors. According to representatives of Freeman's creditors, Amis's lawsuit was just another means of concealing Freeman's property.[23]

I do not know whether Robert Mott's accusations were rooted in reality, but there is sufficient evidence to suggest that at least some members of Theophilus Freeman's community believed they were. Junius Amis's lawsuit against the Bank of Kentucky was neither the first nor the last civil dispute where his and Freeman's interests seem to have been aligned.[24] In the words of Judge Alexander McKenzie Buchanan, who presided over another lawsuit Amis filed against one of Freeman's creditors, "when I consider that I have had of late sitting here as judge of this court occasion to observe numerous examples of business done and collections made by Theophilus Freeman in the name of Junius Amis, I am easily led to the belief that in this as in so many other instances Amis was but another name for Freeman."[25] But whether Amis was actually working to defraud Freeman's creditors is not important; what matters is that Freeman's creditors leveled the same accusations of collusion and fraud against both Amis and Sarah Connor.

Junius Amis lost his lawsuits against Alden F. Dunbar and the Bank of Kentucky. He was not only unable to regain possession of Isam and Emmanuel but was also ordered to pay Theophilus's creditors damages. But whatever the nature of Freeman's and Amis's relationship, the consequences of Amis's supposed fraud did not extend beyond his pocketbook and were arguably never as costly as those endured by Sarah Connor, whose exploits in New Orleans courts were ultimately at the expense of her freedom.

A. A. Fraser, Alden F. Dunbar's attorney, and Robert Mott, representing the Bank of Kentucky, penned near-identical responses to Sarah Connor's lawsuits. Fraser asked the Fifth District Court of New Orleans to dismiss Connor's claims, as she was "a slave and the property of Theophilus Freeman," unable to "file a petition or take a rule in a court of justice." Robert Mott included the same sentence in his response to Connor's lawsuit against the Bank of Kentucky. According to Mott and Fraser, Freeman fraudulently freed Connor after he became insolvent and had since carried on "a considerable traffic in slaves" in Connor's name in order to defraud his creditors.[26]

Robert Mott and A. A. Fraser's accusations were not necessarily unique. Judith Kelleher Schafer argued that while free people of color in New Orleans had certain rights, they also had "serious legal disabilities" as their freedom was always potentially subject to question.[27] Twenty years before Sarah Connor sued the Bank of Kentucky and Alden F. Dunbar, Isabella Hawkins found herself in a similar situation. On March 13, 1827, Hawkins, a free woman of color and resident of Pointe Coupee Parish, Louisiana, filed a lawsuit against parish sheriff Stephen Van Wickle. Hawkins alleged that Van Wickle had wrongfully repossessed her property—an enslaved woman named Milly, four horses, and two cows—to compensate for John M. Walker's debts. Walker was Hawkins's former owner. Stephen Van Wickle's attorneys, Turner and Johnson, relied on Hawkins's race to undermine her claims, arguing that Hawkins was "not able or capable in law to institute or prosecute this action" because she was "a slave as appears by her color which is black." With that, Hawkins became a plaintiff in a property dispute *and* a freedom suit.[28] Isabella Hawkins and Sarah Connor could file civil suits, but because they were women of color, opposing attorneys could undermine their respective claims and endanger their statuses as free women by questioning whether they were free or enslaved.

In addition to questioning whether Sarah Connor was a free woman, Fraser and Mott accused Connor of pursuing Mary Ann and Ellen at Freeman's behest, labeling her as Freeman's slave, concubine, and tool. While Connor and Freeman consistently denied they conspired to commit fraud, they did so without discussing their relationship. For Fraser and Mott, arguing that Connor and Freeman lived together "in a state of concubinage" bolstered their respective claims that the two were in cahoots; it was also of legal significance. Louisiana's laws prevented "free white persons" from marrying "free people of color" but still regulated these relationships—specifically in regard to illegitimate children, grounds for divorce, and property.[29] Article 1468 of Louisiana's Civil Code states that "those who have lived together in open concubinage" could transfer money or property to one another only if the value transferred did not "exceed one-tenth part of the whole value of their estate."[30] If Mott's and Fraser's strategy of undermining Sarah Connor's status as a free woman failed, they might then rely on Article 1468 to argue that Freeman had illegally transferred his assets to Connor.

None of the regulations that the state of Louisiana imposed on those who lived together "in open concubinage" applied to either party's ability to act as a plaintiff or defendant in civil court. Conversely, a legally married woman's access to Louisiana's courts was explicitly tied to her spouse, as a married woman could not "appear in court" without her husband's permission. Louisiana's Civil Code did, however, provide married women with a means of independently managing and protecting their individual property from their husbands. Louisiana distinguished between a married woman's dotal property—money and property the wife brought to her husband in order to "assist him in bearing the expenses"—and extra-dotal or paraphernal property, which belonged to a married woman individually and was explicitly not included in her dowry.[31] A married woman in Louisiana was thus able to manage her paraphernal property "without the assistance of her husband." When a husband mismanaged his wife's individual property, she was free to sue him, as she possessed, "even during marriage, a right of action against her husband for the restitution of her paraphernal effects."[32]

Although a marriage contract did not bind Sarah Connor and Theophilus Freeman, their relationship and the workings of New Orleans courts did.[33] After suing Freeman for her freedom in 1846, Connor was a legally free, unmarried woman, independent of her former owner, who was not legally required to seek his permission to exercise the privileges that her freedom afforded her. In reality, however, living with Freeman "in a state of concubinage" shaped both the circumstances of Connor's freedom and her ability to maneuver within the space of a courtroom. Because all we can learn about Connor and Freeman's relationship comes from court records, we can never know whether or to what extent Freeman was pulling Connor's strings. We know that when Connor set foot in a courtroom, she depended on Freeman to affirm that she was a free woman, as her successful suit against him was consistently deemed insufficient evidence of her freedom. But the fact that Freeman usually supported Connor's efforts in court does not mean he did not possess power that he could have wielded over her outside the courtroom and during their relationship. With a simple refusal, he could not only undermine Connor's claim to her enslaved property but also endanger her legal status as a free woman. Connor knew it, and Freeman did, too. Although he was not technically her owner, his decisions and debts shaped and constrained her ability to use the privileges her freedom afforded her.

Connor needed Freeman's support in court. She also needed to distance herself from him to present herself as an individual plaintiff. It was not the letter of the law that bound her to Freeman. Robert Mott and A. A. Fraser's claims that Connor was Freeman's concubine and tool effectively undermined her status as an individual plaintiff by connecting her actions as an enslaver to her former owner. She was no longer his legal property, but she still had to work to disentangle herself from

Freeman when she sued his creditors. The experience must have been frustrating. Even though she could access New Orleans courts as an individual plaintiff in a property dispute—a privilege reserved for free individuals—the ways that others used her connection to Freeman to undermine Connor likely served as a chilling reminder that she was not so far removed from the circumstances of her enslavement.

To support her claim that she was Mary Ann and Ellen's "true and lawful owner" and to refute Mott and Fraser's accusations that she was Freeman's slave and tool that he was using to defraud his creditors, Connor relied on documentary evidence and testimony. In *Connor, f.w.c. v. The Bank of Kentucky* (1848), Connor presented two acts of sale as evidence and also called on Caroline M. Williams, Melissa Garrison, Jacob Tosspot, and Fanny Preston to testify on her behalf. The witnesses responded to questions regarding Mary Ann and Ellen, Connor's freedom, and Connor's relationship with Freeman. Caroline Williams, a white woman, widow, and resident of Natchez, Mississippi, who previously owned Mary Ann and Ellen, was deposed before Adams County justice of the peace Jacob A. Van Hoesen on May 12, 1848. She testified that she was "acquainted with Sarah Connor," explaining she sold Mary Ann to Connor on May 19, 1847, and in another transaction with Connor exchanged Ellen for an enslaved man named Lewis on December 20 of the same year. When asked whether it was Theophilus Freeman who actually purchased Mary Ann and Ellen, Caroline responded, "Sarah made all the transactions and bargains herself." Furthermore, "Freeman or no one else [was] acting for said Sarah."[34]

On July 12, 1848, Melissa Garrison, Jacob Tosspot, and Fanny Preston were deposed before Justice of the Peace George Y. Bright in New Orleans. Garrison, Tosspot, and Preston were free people of color, residents of New Orleans, and likely friends of Sarah Connor. Unlike Caroline M. Williams, they did not discuss Mary Ann or Ellen; instead, they responded to questions regarding Connor's freedom and Theophilus Freeman. Garrison testified that she met Connor in 1840 and recounted how Connor had worked until she secured enough money to purchase her freedom. Jacob Tosspot and Fanny Preston described how they became acquainted with Connor and Theophilus Freeman five years earlier in Cincinnati. Tosspot recalled that Connor, then in the company of Freeman, "acted as a free woman" while in the city. Preston confirmed that Connor was "regarded as a free woman" in Cincinnati and explained that Connor boarded with her in Cincinnati for some weeks before returning to New Orleans with Freeman.

While records from *Connor, f.w.c. v. The Bank of Kentucky* (1848) do not include the questions Robert Mott asked Melissa Garrison, Jacob Tosspot, and Fanny Preston, their responses suggest that Mott did not limit his questions to issues relating to Sarah Connor. In addition to explaining how they knew Connor was a free woman, Garrison, Tosspot, and Preston were asked to offer personal information. Garrison testified that she was born Melissa Farrington and that a Baptist preacher by the name of Flint presided over her wedding to her husband, William Garrison, on September 7, 1844, in Mount Pleasant, Ohio. When she was deposed in July 1848, Garrison was living at "Mrs. Hickey's," located on Gravier Street in New Orleans, "between Baronne and Carondolet Streets, on the left hand side as you walk toward the river." Tosspot's and Preston's recorded responses to Mott's questions were relatively brief compared to Garrison's extensive answers. Tosspot's testimony was documented as follows: "I am a free colored man. I was born in the State of Virginia. I live in New Orleans." Similarly, Preston testified that she was a "colored woman" and "was born in the State of Virginia."[35] Their responses suggest that Connor, as a plaintiff, was not the only person whose freedom was in question when she entered a courtroom; some free people of color who acted as witnesses may also have been on the receiving end of questions regarding their status when they testified in court.

As an attorney representing the Bank of Kentucky, Robert Mott worked to discredit witnesses who supported Sarah Connor's claim to Mary Ann and Ellen. Because Melissa Garrison, Jacob Tosspot, and Fanny Preston were people of color, Mott questioned their ability to act as witnesses by asking them to recount specific details regarding their personal lives and to establish their freedom. *Connor v. The Bank of Kentucky* (1848) marks the only time that a person of color testified on Connor's behalf. As many of the original court records from *Connor, f.w.c. v. Dunbar* (1848) have been lost, it is possible that Garrison, Tosspot, and Preston testified in that lawsuit as well. It stands to reason, however, that just as Robert Mott could undermine a witness in court based on the witness's race, Sarah Connor's attorneys could also make a calculated decision to call on witnesses whose status as free individuals was never subject to question: white men.

Connor, f.w.c. v. The Bank of Kentucky (1848) would remain unresolved until 1854, but Mary Ann and Ellen were sold in June 1849. R. S. Moss purchased Mary Ann and then sold her to Samuel Powers, and Nicholas Johnson purchased Ellen. In August of that year, Sarah Connor filed two lawsuits in the Third District Court of New Orleans, the first, against Moss, and the second, against Johnson and Powers. Although records from *Connor, f.w.c. v. Moss* (1848) and *Connor, f.w.c. v. Powers and Johnson* (1848) have been lost, Samuel Powers's testimony in a subsequent lawsuit involving Connor offers some insight into the recurring challenges she faced as a plaintiff.

On January 16, 1850, Samuel Powers testified on behalf of the plaintiff in *A.F. Dunbar v. Connor, f.w.c.* (1849). Powers testified that he had "seen Freeman and Sarah in bed together" and mused that while "they live together as man and wife but as to who pays the rent, he cannot tell." He described his legal strategy in *Connor, f.w.c. v. Powers and Johnson* (1849), then pending in the Third District Court of New Orleans. He explained that he had "alleged in his defense to said suit that she, Sarah, is not a free woman." Additionally, he "always felt confident that Sarah Connor had no right to the suit" and believed she "would discontinue the suit but that Freeman would not permit her."[36]

Powers's testimony tells us that the challenges Connor faced in her lawsuits against the Bank of Kentucky and Alden F. Dunbar were not unique. By simply questioning whether she was a free woman, acting independently of her former owner, Powers succeeded in making Connor into a plaintiff who was responsible not only for supporting her original claim but also for defending her freedom and presenting herself as an individual plaintiff and property owner. The acts of sale that Connor presented to demonstrate that she was Mary Ann's and Ellen's lawful owner as well as her previous freedom suit against Theophilus Freeman were not sufficient evidence of her freedom. The evidentiary standards she encountered by simply acting as a plaintiff or defendant were not only legal or archival, they were also racial and gendered. While not every free person of color who filed a civil suit was forced into the same precarious situation, every free person of color who filed a lawsuit *could* be compelled to establish and defend his or her freedom. Connor could act as a plaintiff in a civil suit, but her race and gender made her vulnerable when she set foot inside a courtroom.

The Defendant

On July 11, 1848, Robert Mott, representing the Bank of Kentucky, filed a lawsuit against Sarah Connor and Theophilus Freeman in the Fifth District Court of New Orleans. Mott accused Freeman of fraudulently freeing Connor to protect her from his creditors and argued that the proceedings from *Connor, f.w.c. v. Freeman* (1846) were "illegal." Mott asked the court to reverse that decision, which had freed Connor, and to declare that she was Freeman's slave, subject to seizure and sale to compensate for his debts. This marked the first of two lawsuits in which Freeman's creditors explicitly asked the Fifth District Court of New Orleans to revoke Connor's freedom; A. A. Fraser would file the second on Alden F. Dunbar's behalf in May 1849.

Connor and Freeman spent much of the next three years defending themselves against accusations of fraud, but only Connor faced the possibility of enslavement. The fact that Freeman's creditors were able to convince the court to declare that Connor was a slave speaks to the tenuous nature of her freedom. When Junius Amis lost his lawsuits against the Bank of Kentucky and Alden F. Dunbar, he paid court costs and damages, and neither party filed a countersuit. When Connor did the same, Freeman's creditors made her into a defendant in a freedom suit and convinced the courts that she was a slave. Considering the consequences of Connor's perceived fraud alongside the consequences that Amis experienced suggests that Connor's continued presence in the courtroom made her vulnerable. Each time she tried to use the law as other enslavers did, to challenge their rivals or protect their investments in enslaved property, she was in a position where others could use the law to threaten her freedom and, eventually, make her into a slave.

Sarah Connor's responses to the Bank of Kentucky and Alden F. Dunbar's respective lawsuits were one and the same. She recounted the details of how she secured her freedom via self-purchase, explaining "she was never the slave of Theophilus Freeman"; rather, she negotiated her sale in order to secure her emancipation. According to Connor, she paid the $750 that Freeman used to purchase her from Jane Shelton, and all parties involved agreed that the transaction was made "for her benefit" and with the understanding that it would lead to her emancipation. Furthermore, Connor argued, she had lived as a free woman long before Freeman became insolvent, as she had "purchased and sold property [including] slaves and movables" as well as "visited frequently the free states, residing several months at a time in the free cities of Philadelphia, New York, and Cincinnati." Finally, Connor denied "having been the means used by Freeman to defraud his creditors or to conceal his property, on the contrary," she claimed, "your respondent at this time is a creditor of Freeman to a large amount."

Connor's defense was fairly straightforward: she argued that she could not be Freeman's property because she became a free woman the moment he purchased her from Jane Shelton. Connor could travel, buy and sell property, and be recognized as a plaintiff and defendant in New Orleans courts. She thus drew on documentary evidence and testimony to relay the instances when she was recognized as a free woman and had exercised the privileges that the law afforded free women of color in Louisiana.

Connor called on witnesses to support her claim that she had purchased her freedom and had traveled, with Theophilus Freeman's consent, to northern states where slavery was illegal. H. J. Ranney, Mark Davis, and John L. Harris, three white men who were acquainted with Connor, corroborated her claim that she and Freeman had spent months in New York City in 1841 and in Cincinnati in 1843. For Connor, establishing that Freeman had consented to her travels after purchasing her from Jane Shelton was of the utmost importance.

Enslaved women in Louisiana who sued for their freedom on the grounds that they had resided in states where slavery was illegal also worked to establish that their respective owners had allowed them to travel. In December 1822, an enslaved woman named Rebecca Lunsford sued L. Coquillon, her owner, for her freedom in the First District Court of Louisiana. Lunsford claimed that some years earlier, her previous owner, James Riddle, took her to Cincinnati, where she remained in his family's service for several years. When she attempted to claim she was free, Riddle forcibly took her to Kentucky, where he sold her southward to New Orleans. After several witnesses confirmed that Lunsford had indeed spent several months in Ohio, with Riddle's consent, Judge Joshua Lewis ruled in Lunsford's favor, a decision the Louisiana Supreme Court would confirm on appeal.[37]

Although James Riddle was no longer Rebecca Lunsford's owner, his consent was still instrumental in her efforts to secure her freedom in a Louisiana courtroom. According to Judith K. Schafer, the verdict in *Lunsford, f.w.c. v. Coquillon* (1824) was consistent with the Louisiana Supreme Court's decisions in cases "involving transportation to a free state or country" throughout the antebellum period.[38] It was not until Louisiana's legislature passed "an Act to Protect the Rights of Slaveholders in the State of Louisiana" in May 1846 that the court's tendency to side with the enslaved plaintiff would begin to change. The act stated, "no slave shall be entitled to his or her freedom, under the pretense that he or she has been, with or without the consent of his or her owner, in a country where slavery does not exist, or in any of the States where slavery is prohibited."[39] Because Sarah Connor ventured northward with Theophilus Freeman's permission in as early as 1841, this particular path to emancipation was still accessible at the time.

Once again, Connor was forced to rely on Freeman to prove that she was free. She also depended on testimony and evidence to demonstrate that others and the state of Louisiana had recognized her as a free woman. She presented a notarial contract, dated December 8, 1842, that documented her sale of a 10-year-old enslaved child, Emily, to Evariste Blanc, a resident of New Orleans. On that day, Connor appeared before New Orleans notary William Christy, who recognized her as a free woman of color, capable of owning, buying, and selling enslaved property. As the state of Louisiana had effectively recognized Connor's freedom more than two years before Freeman became insolvent, his creditors had no claim to Connor as a slave. Connor's attorney also pointed to her ability to act as a plaintiff in court as further evidence that the state and Freeman's creditors had recognized her freedom. The attorney argued that because Alden F. Dunbar had "contested with her in this honorable court, in the suit 1193, as a free woman, her right of property to two slaves, Mary Ann and Ellen," he had already acknowledged that she was a free woman, not Freeman's enslaved property.

Sarah Connor's self-purchase, property, mobility, and access to New Orleans courts were ultimately insufficient evidence of her freedom. Judge Alexander McKenzie Buchanan ruled in favor of the plaintiffs in *The Bank of Kentucky v. Connor, f.w.c. et al.* (1848) and *Dunbar, et al. v. Connor, f.w.c., et al.* (1849), declaring Connor "the property of Theophilus Freeman and subject as such to execution in favor of the plaintiffs." Connor would successfully appeal both decisions before the Louisiana Supreme Court between 1849 and 1851. Connor, no doubt weary from years of fending off Freeman's creditors, included the following in a letter to the Louisiana Supreme Court dated May 18, 1850: "My freedom which I have enjoyed before all the city for ten years past is involved in the pursuit of the Creditors of a person who formerly had a title to me." In its written decision, the court found a similar disconnect between Alden F. Dunbar and the Bank of Kentucky's claims and Connor's status, calling her an "industrious thrifty woman" who desired her freedom and "worked hard to effect that object."[40]

Justices of the Louisiana Supreme Court agreed that Theophilus Freeman had treated Sarah Connor "as a free person" since 1841, citing evidence of her travels with his consent to Cincinnati and New York before Freeman became insolvent. Furthermore, as the Bank of Kentucky and Alden F. Dunbar were not among the parties involved in Connor's freedom suit, they had "no right to ask that the judgment be declared null and void." Freeman's issues with his creditors and the fact that Connor sued him for her freedom after he became insolvent "ought not to alter any bona fide rights which Sarah [Connor] the defendant had acquired." On January 13, 1851, the Supreme Court of Louisiana ordered that the Fifth District Court of New Orleans's decisions in favor of the plaintiffs in *The Bank of Kentucky v. Connor, f.w.c.* (1848) and *Dunbar, et al. v. Connor, f.w.c. et al.* (1849) be reversed in favor of the defendant.[41]

Once again, Sarah Connor entered a New Orleans courtroom enslaved and left as a free woman in the eyes of the state of Louisiana. She did not, however, enjoy her legal status as a free woman or as a resident of New Orleans for much longer. From 1830 well into the 1850s, Louisiana's legislature passed several acts to prevent free people of color from remaining in the state.[42] In 1849, while Alden F. Dunbar and the Bank of Kentucky were working steadily to convince the Fifth District Court of New Orleans to declare that Connor was a slave, Connor was petitioning the City of New Orleans to allow her to remain a resident. Her requests were rejected four times between 1849 and 1851. Aldermen Etter, who presided over New Orleans's Second Municipality Council in August 1851 and who rejected Connor's last petition, noted that previous committees had "examined minutely into the character of the petitioner [Sarah], and find it not at all reputable." While Connor was a free woman, Etter concluded, and the "action of a municipal Council is not necessary to perfect that freedom," the council's action was "necessary to permit her to remain in the State." On August 7, 1851, just eight months after the Louisiana Supreme Court restored Connor's freedom, Alderman Etter ordered Sarah Connor to "leave the State of Louisiana within sixty days of legal notice."[43]

Two days later, on August 9, 1851, Sarah Connor once again appeared before Alderman Etter, this time, to answer to a charge of perjury.[44] In July of that year, Sarah signed an affidavit in which she accused Charles Cammayer, May Ann Cunningham, and Mary Ann Cunningham of stealing and harboring her enslaved property, a man by the name of Peter. When the courts decided that Connor was mistaken, she was charged with perjury in the First District Court of New Orleans alongside Theophilus Freeman, who was charged with subornation of perjury. The First District Court, which prioritized criminal trials but also heard civil suits from time to time, heard some 1,300 trials and lawsuits in 1851.

Connor and Freeman were two of three individuals tried for perjury that year.[45] Although it was Connor, not Freeman, who accused a white man and two white women of stealing Peter, the district attorney thought it fitting to charge them both, explaining, "Sarah Connor was only the tool of a white man named Freeman who lived with her." On April 3, 1852, Connor was convicted of perjury and sentenced to "five years imprisonment at hard labor in the State penitentiary."[46]

Freedom

Sarah Connor unsuccessfully appealed the First District Court of Louisiana's decision to the Louisiana Supreme Court in June 1852.[47] However, because reports from the Louisiana State Penitentiary make no mention of Connor, it is uncertain whether she ever spent any time in prison. During the 1850s, the penitentiary's board of directors published annual reports that included detailed information about each prisoner; Sarah Connor was never mentioned. While her absence may reflect a clerical error, the fact that she was able to continue appearing in New Orleans courts as late as 1854 suggests that Connor may have avoided imprisonment for some time, if not indefinitely.[48]

Proceedings in *Connor, f.w.c. v. The Bank of Kentucky* (1848) dragged on until May 1854, when Judge M. M. Reynolds of the Fourth District Court of New Orleans ruled in favor of the defendant and ordered Sarah Connor to pay the Bank of Kentucky more than $1,500, plus damages and court costs.[49] Judge Reynolds's ruling marked the end of Connor's time in New Orleans's courts in the 1850s, as she does not appear to have filed another civil suit until June 1874.[50] That is not to say that Connor stopped working to protect her enslaved property—only that her experiences with Theophilus Freeman's creditors taught her that the risks of entering New Orleans's courtrooms to do so outweighed its potential rewards.

On July 17, 1854, Orleans Parish sheriff's deputy J. Walden seized a 30-year-old enslaved woman named Diana to compensate for Sarah Connor's outstanding debt to the Bank of Kentucky. Connor did not attempt to regain possession of Diana by filing a lawsuit. On August 23,

1854, Diana was transported from the local jail to the City Exchange Hotel, located at the corner of Chartres and Royal Street. At noon, she was led to an auction block at the center of a large rotunda and auctioned off to the highest bidder. Smith Isard, a white man, agreed to pay $1,465 cash for Diana, and she became his enslaved property. I do not know whether Connor was present when Diana was sold, but as Isard purchased her on Connor's behalf, she likely found no reason to attend the auction herself.[51]

Sarah Connor lived with Smith Isard in New Orleans from at least 1860 until Isard's death in November 1872.[52] When Connor and Theophilus Freeman stopped living together remains unclear. Freeman did, however, attempt to claim Connor as his slave in July 1852. While his attempt was unsuccessful, his efforts demonstrate that his years of supporting Connor's efforts to claim her legal freedom in court did little to sever the ties between them. The fact that he believed he could convince a court that Connor was his property some six years after she won her freedom suit suggests that he was well aware of and capable of exercising his power over her.[53]

When Connor sued Freeman's creditors, was she acting of her own volition? Was Freeman pulling the strings? We cannot know for certain. The documentary evidence Connor relied on to prove she was a free woman and to support her claims to Mary Ann and Ellen may have been a site of her oppression and continued subjugation to her former owner. Freeman could have orchestrated Connor's actions as an enslaver, plaintiff, and defendant. Just as his creditors could call attention to Connor's race and relationship to undermine any evidence of her freedom and claims to Mary Ann and Ellen, Freeman could have done much the same to force Connor into signing bills of sale, creating affidavits, and filing lawsuits. The court records that allow us a glimpse of Sarah Connor's life hint at the complicated nature of her freedom but tell us little in the way of its daily realities. What these records do make clear, however, is that even though Connor was free on paper, and even if she was telling the truth when she claimed Mary Ann and Ellen were her property, lawyers could demonstrate she was "only the tool of a white man" without any documentary evidence to support their claims. In court, it was all too easy to convince judges and juries that a free woman of color's well-evidenced claim was indicative of her ongoing enslavement.

After she passed away in Washington, DC, on May 7, 1892, Sarah Connor's body was transported to New Orleans, where she was buried in Cypress Grove Cemetery in lot number 181, beside Smith Isard. The inscription on her headstone reads as follows: "Sarah Ann Connor, wife of Smith L. Isard, Born in Fairfax Co., Virginia. Died in Washington D.C. May 7, 1892, aged 72 years."[54]

Between 1841 and 1854, Sarah Ann Connor worked diligently to secure and defend her freedom and property in court. Her decision to not sue to regain possession of Diana, as she did in her pursuit of Mary Ann and Ellen, suggests that her experiences as a plaintiff and defendant forced her to recognize that the courtroom could be a dangerous place. Rather than risk her freedom, she looked to Smith Isard, a white man, to purchase her enslaved property for her. While it was Connor's choice to never enter a courtroom to protect her enslaved property again, it was a decision that her experiences in New Orleans courts compelled her to make. It was not the letter of the law but its racial and gendered workings that ultimately defined the possibilities and limits of her freedom.

Conclusion

I TELL MY STUDENTS that everything a historian writes is their argument for how history should be written. This book is mine, and this conclusion is for them.

I've struggled with how to end this. Should I tell one more story? Make one more point and walk away? Finally, thankfully, I have arrived at the conclusion that all I want to talk about, the only person I really want to talk about, is John.

I still don't know where he was born. I can't tell you where he died. I don't know where his people were, what he dreamed about, or where he most wanted to be. Still, I believe each chapter of this book contributes something to our understanding of what was possible in the world John lived in. In the circumstances of Isaac Wright's enslavement, we see a business in which repetition, deception, and constructing the past were essential, dreadful parts. In working to reconstruct the last year of Jack Smith's life, we learn that enslaved people were most always at the center of the past that enslavers worked to construct—perhaps not always powerful or autonomous, but always present and important. In Betsey's enslavement, we find a possible history of every enslaved person who appears and disappears in a contract. And in Sarah Ann Connor's efforts to make and keep herself free, we find the uncodified limits of the world that shaped John's life and constrained his choices.

In some ways, we are where we began: a name, an age, a sex, and a price. The limits of John's history are real and unyielding, but its possibilities are ours to identify and give shape. For historians, there is always a space between the story we want to tell and the story we get to tell. I have used questions about historical production and knowledge to try to make sense of enslaved people's experiences at the center of a narrative they did not choose. In doing so, I have put them at the center of another narrative that they never could have chosen. I have sifted through written records that were central to their exploitation and commodification, and I, too, have made demands of their pasts. To what end have I told these stories? It is my sincere hope that in telling them, I have in some way contributed to the ever-growing evidence that intellectual histories of enslaved people are possible and valuable to our understanding not only of the business of slavery but also of American history. It is my hope that historians of enslaved people continue to do the important work of looking for the enslaved in well-trodden records where we have been told these individuals are silent. And it is my hope that we continue to work to learn from the past in the interest of building a better, more equitable present.

This book not only demonstrates that enslavers cared about what was written down but also shows us that enslaved people's histories were always a site of their commodification. I believe that in acknowledging that enslaved people are at the center of the record of antebellum slavery, we must also recognize that there is most always a way to center the enslaved in our scholarship. And it is important that we do so, because in working to historicize the human beings who were the focus of enslavers' archival constructions, we also do the difficult, important work of resisting enslavers' control, not of the lives of the enslaved, but of the stories we get to tell about slavery. And it matters that we resist enslavers' efforts to control the narrative because enslaved people's histories are worth fighting for. Although history cannot remedy the irreparable violence of the slavers' archive, it can create a physical analog to the written record, generating a new way of encountering individuals such as

John—one that acknowledges what we cannot know while also working to learn what we can. We pick up the pieces to wrest control of the historical narrative from the hands of enslavers—as a means of using stories to ends that enslavers tried to refuse and deny.

Finally, it is a cliché that knowledge is power, but it is also true. In defining thousands of people by a first name, an age, a sex, and a price, enslavers did the careful, deliberate work of historical production and erasure, controlling access to much of the information available to historians for the purposes of making or saving a few bucks. While we do not have to tell the stories they wanted told, we are nevertheless bound by their decisions. This means that the choices we make today—"about who lives and who doesn't," about whose stories are told and privileged—matter now and will matter in the future. We may not have infinite power over the data and information that fill our world, but we do have the ability to choose the lessons we wish to learn and unlearn. Is there anything lovelier and more filled with possibility than asking a question and working to answer it?[1]

Introduction

1. I rely heavily on the insights of scholars who have worked to understand the power dynamics of the archive in their efforts to historicize enslaved and disenfranchised people, including but not limited to the following: James C. Scott, *Weapons of the Weak: Everyday Forms of Peasant Resistance* (New Haven, CT: Yale University Press, 1985); Natalie Zemon Davis, *Fiction in the Archives: Pardon Tales and Their Tellers in Sixteenth-Century France* (Stanford, CA: Stanford University Press, 1987); Hortense J. Spillers, "Mama's Baby, Papa's Maybe: An American Grammar Book," *Diacritics* 17 (Summer 1987): 64–81; James C. Scott, *Domination and the Arts of Resistance: Hidden Transcripts* (New Haven, CT: Yale University Press, 1990); Michel-Rolph Trouillot, *Silencing the Past: Power and the Production of History* (Boston: Beacon Press, 1995); Walter Johnson, "Inconsistency, Contradiction, and Complete Confusion: The Everyday Life of the Law of Slavery," *Law and Social Inquiry* 22 (April 1997): 405–433; Walter Johnson, "Time and Revolution in African America," *Black Renaissance* 3 (Summer–Fall 2001): 83–101; Walter Johnson, "On Agency," *Journal of Social History* 37 (2003): 113–124; Joyce E. Chaplin, *Subject Matter: Technology, the Body, and Science on the Anglo-American Frontier, 1500–1676* (Cambridge, MA: Harvard University Press, 2003); Katherine McKittrick, *Demonic Grounds: Black Women and the Cartographies of Struggle* (Minneapolis: University of Minnesota Press, 2006); Joseph Calder Miller, *The Problem of Slavery as History: A Global Approach* (New Haven, CT: Yale University Press, 2012); Katherine McKittrick, "Mathematics of Black Life," *Black Scholar* 44 (2014): 16–28; Anthony E. Kaye, "The Problem of Autonomy: Toward a Postliberal History," in *New Directions in Slavery Studies: Commodification, Community, and Comparison*, ed. Jeff Forret and Christine E. Sears (Baton Rouge: Louisiana State University Press, 2015); Marisa J. Fuentes and Brian Connolly, "Introduction: From Archives of Slavery to Liberated Futures?," *History of the Present* 6 (Fall 2016): 105–116; Stephanie E. Smallwood, "The Politics of the Archive and History's Accountability to the Enslaved," *History of the Present* 6 (Fall 2016): 117–132; David Kazanjian, "Freedom's Surprise: Two Paths Through Slavery's Archives," *History of the Present* 6 (Fall 2016): 133–145; Marisa J. Fuentes, *Dispossessed Lives: Enslaved Women, Violence, and the Archive* (Philadelphia: University of Pennsylvania Press, 2016).

2. Here, I aim to do the work necessary to, in the words of Saidiya Hartman, "exceed or negotiate the constitutive limits of the archive," not by making assumptions or claiming to know what cannot be known, but by interrogating the nature of the

written record with an eye toward what is possible and impossible to learn. "This double gesture," Hartman explains, "can be described as straining against the limits of the archive to write a cultural history of the captive, and, at the same time, enacting the impossibility of representing the lives of the captives precisely through the process of narration." Saidiya Hartman, "Venus in Two Acts," *Small Axe* 26 (June 2008): 11. In this endeavor, I am deeply indebted to Michel-Rolph Trouillot, Saidiya Hartman, Marisa J. Fuentes, and Jennifer L. Morgan—scholars who, in their willingness to contemplate how we can and should write history, have helped historians of the enslaved work toward reconciling our shared goal of writing histories that center enslaved people with our reliance on an archive their enslavers created. Michel-Rolph Trouillot, *Silencing the Past: Power and the Production of History* (Boston: Beacon Press, 1995); Saidiya Hartman, *Scenes of Subjection: Terror, Slavery, and Self-Making in Nineteenth-Century America* (Oxford: Oxford University Press, 1997); Hartman, "Venus in Two Acts," 6; Saidiya Hartman, *Lose Your Mother: A Journey Along the Atlantic Slave Route* (New York: Farrar, Straus and Giroux, 2007); Saidiya Hartman, "The Dead Book Revisited," *History of the Present: A Journal of Critical History* 6 (Fall 2016): 208–215; Jennifer L. Morgan, "Accounting for 'the Most Excruciating Torment': Gender, Slavery, and Trans-Atlantic Passages," *History of the Present: A Journal of Critical History* 6 (Fall 2016): 184–207; Jennifer L. Morgan, *Reckoning with Slavery: Gender, Kinship, and Capitalism in the Early Black Atlantic* (Durham, NC: Duke University Press, 2021).

3. Lawrence J. Kotlikoff, "The Structure of Slave Prices in New Orleans, 1804 to 1862," *Economic Inquiry* 17 (1979): 496–518; Herman Freudenberger and Jonathan B. Pritchett, "The Domestic United States Slave Trade: New Evidence," *Journal of Interdisciplinary History* 21 (Winter 1991): 447–477.

4. Gatlin v. Kendig, No. 13731, Fourth District Court of New Orleans, New Orleans, March 1860. This book contributes to the extensive literature on the slave trade in the antebellum United States. For more on New Orleans and the domestic slave trade in the nineteenth-century United States, see the following: Michael Tadman, *Speculators and Slaves: Masters, Traders, and Slaves in the Old South* (Madison: University of Wisconsin Press, 1989); Ira Berlin, *Many Thousands Gone: The First Two Centuries of Slavery in North America* (Cambridge, MA: Harvard University Press, 1998); Walter Johnson, *Soul by Soul: Life Inside the Antebellum Slave Market* (Cambridge: Harvard University Press, 1999); Robert H. Gudmestad, *A Troublesome Commerce: Transformation of the Interstate Slave Trade* (Baton Rouge: Louisiana State University Press, 2003); Steven Deyle, *Carry Me Back: The Domestic Slave Trade in American Life* (New York: Oxford University Press, 2005); Walter Johnson, *River of Dark Dreams: Slavery and Empire in the Cotton Kingdom* (Cambridge, MA: Belknap Press, 2013); Scott P. Marler, *The Merchants' Capital: New Orleans and the Political Economy of the Nineteenth-Century South* (Cambridge: Cambridge University Press, 2013); Damian Alan Pargas, *Slavery and Forced Migration in the Antebellum South* (Cambridge: Cambridge University Press, 2014); Calvin Schermerhorn, *The Business of Slavery and the Rise of American Capitalism, 1815–1860* (New Haven, CT: Yale University Press, 2015); Joshua D. Rothman, *The Ledger and the Chain: How Domestic Slave Traders Shaped America* (New York: Basic Books, 2021).

5. Annette Gordon-Reed, *The Hemingses of Monticello: An American Family* (New York: W. W. Norton & Company), 23.

6. I adhere to Walter Johnson's definition of commodification: "In the traders' tables, human beings were fully fungible: any slave, anywhere, could be compared to any other, anywhere else. That was commodification: the distant and different translated into money value and resolved into a single scale of relative prices." Johnson, *Soul by Soul*, 58.

7. This book brings together important conversations on how enslaved people experienced their commodification with the emerging discourse on archival violence. I especially draw inspiration from scholars of the Atlantic world, including the following: Fuentes, *Dispossessed Lives*; Jessica Marie Johnson, *Wicked Flesh: Black Women, Intimacy, and Freedom in the Atlantic World* (Philadelphia: University of Pennsylvania Press, 2020); Morgan, *Reckoning with Slavery*.

8. Hartman, "Venus in Two Acts," 6. This book contributes to the rich and growing literature on how enslaved people experienced their commodification. For more on how enslaved people experienced their commodification, see the following: Daina Ramey Berry, *The Price for Their Pound of Flesh: The Value of the Enslaved from Womb to Grave in the Building of a Nation* (Boston: Beacon Press, 2017); Stephanie E. Jones-Rogers, *They Were Her Property: White Women as Slave Owners in the American South* (New Haven, CT: Yale University Press, 2019); Alexandra J. Finley, *An Intimate Economy: Enslaved Women, Work, and America's Domestic Slave Trade* (Chapel Hill: University of North Carolina Press, 2020); Emily A. Owens, *Consent in the Presence of Force: Sexual Violence and Black Women's Survival in Antebellum New Orleans* (Chapel Hill: University of North Carolina Press, 2023).

9. I lean heavily on the insights of historians who have examined lower civil court records, including but not limited to the following: Ariela J. Gross, *Double Character: Slavery and Mastery in the Antebellum Southern Courtroom* (Athens: University of Georgia Press, 2006); Laura F. Edwards, *The People and Their Peace: Legal Culture and the Transformation of Inequality in the Post-Revolutionary South* (Chapel Hill: University of North Carolina Press, 2009); Anne Twitty, *Before Dred Scott: Slavery and Legal Culture in the American Confluence, 1787–1857* (Cambridge: Cambridge University Press, 2016); Finley, *Intimate Economy*; Owens, *Consent in the Presence of Force*.

10. "Louisiana. First Judicial District Court (Orleans Parish) Records," City Archives, New Orleans Public Library, accessed July 2, 2022, http://archives.nolalibrary .org/~nopl/inv/1jdc/1jdcind.htm.

11. For more on the commodification of enslaved people in the antebellum United States, see the following: Tadman, *Speculators and Slaves*; Richard Holcombe Kilbourne, *Debt, Investment, Slaves: Credit Relations in East Feliciana Parish, Louisiana, 1825–1885* (Tuscaloosa: University of Alabama Press, 1995); Johnson, *Soul by Soul*; Walter Johnson, "The Slave Trader, the White Slave, and the Politics of Racial Determination in the 1850s," *Journal of American History* 87 (2000): 13–38; Edward E. Baptist, "'Cuffy,' 'Fancy Maids,' and 'One-Eyed Men': Rape, Commodification, and the Domestic Slave Trade in the United States," *American Historical Review* 106 (2001): 1619–1650; Robert H. Gudmestad, *A Troublesome Commerce: Transformation of the Interstate Slave Trade* (Baton Rouge: Louisiana State University Press, 2003); Thomas C. Buchanan, *Black Life on the Mississippi: Slaves, Free Blacks, and the Western Steamboat World* (Chapel Hill: University of North Carolina Press, 2004); Deyle, *Carry Me Back*; Johnson, *River of*

Dark Dreams; Marler, *Merchants' Capital*; Edward E. Baptist, *The Half Has Never Been Told: Slavery and the Making of American Capitalism* (New York: Basic Books, 2014); Calvin Schermerhorn, "Slave Trading in a Republic of Credit: Financial Architecture of the US Slave Market, 1815–1840," *Slavery & Abolition* 36 (October 2015): 586–602; Schermerhorn, *Business of Slavery*; Jeff Forret and Christine E. Sears, eds., *New Directions in Slavery Studies: Commodification, Community, and Comparison* (Baton Rouge: Louisiana State University Press, 2015); Rashauna Johnson, *Slavery's Metropolis: Unfree Labor in New Orleans During the Age of Revolutions* (New York: Cambridge University Press, 2016); Sven Beckert and Seth Rockman, eds., *Slavery's Capitalism: A New History of American Economic Development* (Philadelphia: University of Pennsylvania Press, 2016); Ramey Berry, *Price for Their Pound of Flesh*; Caitlin Rosenthal, *Accounting for Slavery: Masters and Management* (Harvard University Press: Cambridge, 2018); Jones-Rogers, *They Were Her Property*; Joshua D. Rothman, *The Ledger and the Chain: How Domestic Slave Traders Shaped America* (New York: Basic Books, 2021); Finley, *Intimate Economy*; Jeff Forret and Bruce E. Baker, eds., *Southern Scoundrels: Grifters and Graft in the Nineteenth Century* (Baton Rouge: Louisiana State University Press, 2021).

12. For more on Louisiana's slave laws, redhibition regulations, and the business of slavery specifically, see the following: Judith K. Schafer, "'Guaranteed Against the Vices and Maladies Prescribed by Law': Consumer Protection, the Law of Slave Sales, and the Supreme Court in Antebellum Louisiana," *American Journal of Legal History* 31, no. 4 (October 1, 1987): 306–321; Andrew Fede, "Legal Protection for Slave Buyers in the U.S. South: A Caveat Concerning Caveat Emptor," *American Journal of Legal History* 31, no. 4 (1987): 322–358; Judith Kelleher Schafer, *Slavery, the Civil Law, and the Supreme Court of Louisiana* (Baton Rouge: Louisiana State University Press, 1994), 127–148; Thomas D. Morris, *Southern Slavery and the Law 1619–1860* (Chapel Hill: University of North Carolina Press, 1996), 112–113; Johnson, *Soul by Soul*, 4, 12–13, 53; Ariela J. Gross, *Double Character: Slavery and Mastery in the Antebellum Southern Courtroom* (Princeton, NJ: Princeton University Press, 2000), 73, 92–93.

13. I rely on the work of scholars who have explored freedom suits as well as those who have interrogated the relationship between enslavement and knowledge production, especially the following: Judith Kelleher Schafer, *Becoming Free, Remaining Free: Manumission and Enslavement in New Orleans, 1846–1862* (Baton Rouge: Louisiana State University Press, 2003); David Thomas Konig, "The Long Road to Dred Scott: Personhood and the Rule of Law in the Trial Court Records of St. Louis Slave Freedom Suits," *University of Missouri–Kansas City Law Review* 75 (Fall 2006): 53–79; Lea VanderVelde, *Redemption Songs: Suing for Freedom Before Dred Scott* (Oxford: Oxford University Press, 2014); Anne Twitty, *Before Dred Scott*, 2016; Kelly M. Kennington, *In the Shadow of Dred Scott: St. Louis Freedom Suits and the Legal Culture of Slavery in Antebellum America* (Athens: University of Georgia Press, 2017); Loren Schweninger, *Appealing for Liberty: Freedom Suits in the South* (Oxford: Oxford University Press, 2018); Morgan, *Reckoning with Slavery*; McKittrick, *Demonic Grounds*.

14. This book builds on and contributes to the work of scholars who have explored the connections between the slave market and the courtroom. Recently, scholars of slavery and capitalism have acknowledged the connections between the business of slavery and the courts, often looking to court records to make sense of the legal and financial risks

involved in the commodification of enslaved property. Jenny Bourne Wahl, *The Bondsman's Burden: An Economic Analysis of the Common Law of Southern Slavery* (Cambridge: Cambridge University Press, 1998), 1–26; Johnson, *Soul by Soul*, 12–13; Thomas C. Buchanan, *Black Life on the Mississippi: Slaves, Free Blacks, and the Western Steamboat World* (Chapel Hill: University of North Carolina Press, 2004), 103–104; Joshua D. Rothman, *Flush Times and Fever Dreams: A Story of Capitalism and Slavery in the Age of Jackson* (Athens: University of Georgia Press, 2012), 9, 53–59; Johnson, *River of Dark Dreams*, 135–150; Baptist, *Half Has Never Been Told*, xxiv, 184–185, 32–35; Schermerhorn, *Business of Slavery*, 4, 62–64, 75–87; Rothman, *Ledger and the Chain*; Finley, *Intimate Economy*; Owens, *Consent in the Presence of Force*, 2023.

1. John and a Bill of Sale

1. For more on Bernard Kendig, see the following: Richard Tansey, "Bernard Kendig and the New Orleans Slave Trade," *Journal of the Louisiana Historical Association* 23, no. 2 (Spring 1982); Jones-Rogers, *They Were Her Property*, 357–362; Maria R. Montalvo, "Bernard Kendig: Orchestrating Fraud in the Market and the Courtroom," in Bruce E. Baker and Jeff Forrett, eds., *Southern Scoundrels: Grifters and Graft in the Nineteenth Century* (Baton Rouge: Louisiana State University Press, 2021). Gatlin v. Kendig, No. 13731, Fourth District Court of New Orleans, New Orleans, March 1860.

2. Hartman, "Venus in Two Acts," 3.

3. Maria R. Montalvo, "The Slavers' Archive: Enslaved People, Power, and the Production of the Past in the Antebellum Courtroom" (PhD diss., Rice University, 2017), 20–64.

4. While Louisiana's redhibition laws were unique in the context of the United States, that was not so in the wider Atlantic world. For more information on how these implied warranty regulations worked elsewhere, see the following: Michelle A. McKinley, *Fractional Freedoms: Slavery, Intimacy, and Legal Mobilization in Colonial Lima, 1600–1700* (Cambridge: Cambridge University Press, 2016), 203–238; Deborah Blumenthal, *Enemies and Familiars: Slavery and Mastery in Fifteenth-Century Valencia* (Ithaca, NY: Cornell University Press, 2009); Judith Kelleher Schafer, "Roman Roots of the Louisiana Law of Slavery: Emancipation in American Louisiana, 1803–1857," *Louisiana Law Review* 56, no. 2 (1996): 409–422.

5. "Immovable things are in general, such as cannot either move themselves or be removed from one place to another. But this definition, strictly speaking, is applicable only to such things as are immovable by their own nature, and not to such as are so only by the disposition of the law." Thomas Gibbes Morgan, *Civil Code of the State of Louisiana: With the Statutory Amendments, from 1825 to 1853, Inclusive; and References to the Decisions of the Supreme Court of Louisiana to the Sixth Volume of Annual Reports* (New Orleans: Bloomfield and Steel, 1854), Book II, Title I, Chapter II, Article 453, p. 71 (hereinafter referred to as the Louisiana Civil Code of 1825). Louisiana's Civil Code made an exception for enslaved people: "Slaves, though movables by their nature, are considered as immovables, by operation of law." Louisiana Civil Code of 1825, Book II, Title I, Chapter II, Article 461, p. 71.

6. According to Article 2415, "All verbal sale of any of these things shall be null, as well for third persons as for the contracting parties themselves, and the testimonial proof

of it shall not be admitted." That is not to say that enslavers never sold enslaved people with verbal agreements alone—only that if and when they did, they could not rely on the state or the courts to help them enforce the terms of their verbal agreements, as Louisiana's civil courts would not accept testimonial proof of the existence of the transaction and its associated obligations. Louisiana Civil Code of 1825, Book III, Title VII, Chapter I, Article 2415, p. 325. According to Article 2231, "The authentic act, as it relates to contracts, is that which has been executed before a notary public or other officer authorized to execute such functions, in presence of two witnesses, free, male, and aged at least fourteen years, or of three witnesses, if the party be blind. If the party does not know how to sign, the notary must cause him to affix his mark to the instrument." According to Article 2233, "The authentic act is full proof of the agreement contained in it, against the contracting parties and their heirs or assigns, unless it be declared and proved a forgery." Louisiana Civil Code of 1825, Book III, Title IV, Chapter VI, Section I, Articles 2231 and 2233, p. 301. Acts under private signature—such as the bill of sale that Bernard Kendig signed—were contracts that were not penned in the presence of a notary (Article 2237). They did not have to be written by the contracting parties, so long as the document was signed by them—meaning, even though parts of Bernard Kendig and Thomas Gatlin's act of sale were printed beforehand, the contract was still valid because it bore Bernard Kendig's signature as well as those of two witnesses (Article 2239).

7. Louisiana Civil Code of 1825, Book III, Title VII, Chapter VI, Article 2450, p. 329.

8. Louisiana Civil Code of 1825, Book III, Title VII, Chapter VI, Article 2451, p. 329.

9. Louisiana Civil Code of 1825, Book III, Title VII, Chapter VI, Section III, Article 2496, p. 334. Technically, Louisiana's redhibition laws applied to any property sold in the state. For example, Louisiana's Civil Code defined the absolute vices of horses and mules as "short wind, glanders and founder." Louisiana Civil Code of 1825, Book III, Title VII, Chapter VI, Section III, Article 2509, p. 336. And while buyers sometimes did sue sellers for redhibition regarding horses or mules they had purchased, enslavers seem to have been far more likely to rely on redhibition suits to cancel sales. This probably has to do with the time constraints the Civil Code placed on lawsuits for redhibition of animals. Article 2513 reads, "The redhibition of animals can only be sued for within fifteen days immediately following the sale." This article was amended in 1828, however, extending the time constraint to two months instead of fifteen days. Even with this amendment, the vast majority of redhibition suits tried before the Orleans Parish Court involved enslaved people. Of the 17,006 civil suits tried before the Orleans Parish Court between 1813 and 1846, 295 were slave-centered redhibition suits, but only 7 were horse-centered redhibition suits. Their case numbers are as follows: 2267, 2579, 3342, 5155, 5195, 6731, and 9524.

10. For more on redhibition laws, specifically as they pertain to the sale of enslaved people in Louisiana, see the following: Schafer, "Guaranteed Against the Vices and Maladies Prescribed by Law'"; Fede, "Legal Protection for Slave Buyers in the U.S. South"; Schafer, *Slavery, the Civil Law, and the Supreme Court of Louisiana*, 127–148; Morris, *Southern Slavery and the Law*, 112–113; Johnson, *Soul by Soul*, 4, 12–13, 53; Gross, *Double Character*, 73, 92–93; Montalvo, "Slavers' Archive," 4–6.

11. "Hidden" defects were defined as those that would not be visible by "simple inspection" at the time of a sale. Dissatisfied buyers took this broad definition and ran

with it, suing sellers over an enslaved person's addiction to drunkenness or suffering from specific diseases or illnesses. Louisiana Civil Code of 1825, Book III, Title VII, Chapter I, Section III, Article 2497, p. 334. Louisiana's Civil Code—from its first promulgation as a digest in 1808 and throughout the remainder of the period when slavery was legal in the state—included six redhibitory vices and defects that were specific to enslaved people. This does not, however, mean that the following six characteristics or illnesses were the only qualities that were the focus of redhibition suits. Louisiana's Civil Code divided redhibitory defects that were specific to enslaved people into two classes: vices of body and vices of character. Vices of body were distinguished further into categories of absolute and relative vices: "Absolute vices are those, of which bare existence gives rise to the redhibitory action; Relative vices are those, which give rise to it, only in proportion to the degree in which they disable the object sold." The absolute vices of enslaved people were leprosy, madness, and epilepsy; the vices of character, "which give rise to the redhibition of slaves, are confined to the cases in which it is proved: That the slave has committed a capital crime; Or, that he is addicted to theft; Or, that he is in the habit of running away. The slave shall be considered as being in the habit of running away, when he shall have absented himself from his master's house twice for several days, or once for more than a month." Louisiana Civil Code of 1825, Book III, Title VII, Chapter VI, Section III, Articles 2501, 2502, 2505.

12. "A declaration made in good faith by the seller, that the thing sold has some quality, which it is found not to have, gives rise to a redhibition, if this quality was the principal motive for making the purchase." Louisiana Civil Code of 1825, Book III, Title VII, Chapter I, Section III, Article 2507, p. 335.

13. J. A. Beard, "Auction Sales," *Daily Picayune* (New Orleans), May 28, 1840, 3.

14. Joseph A. Beard, "Sales at Auction," *Daily Picayune* (New Orleans), August 20, 1840, 3.

15. Joseph A. Beard was a witness in the following civil suit: A. F. Dunbar v. Connor, f.w.c., Fifth District No. 2496, Fifth District Court of New Orleans, New Orleans, May 1849; Dunbar v. Connor, f.w.c., and Freeman, No. 1700, Louisiana Supreme Court, May 1850.

16. For a further discussion of warranty regulations pertaining to slave sales in common law states, see the following: Lee-Carl Overstreet, "Some Aspects of Implied Warranties in the Supreme Court of Missouri," *Missouri Law Review* 10, no. 3 (June 1945): 147–194, 173–175; Morris, *Southern Slavery and the Law*, 109; Wahl, *Bondsman's Burden*, 29–38.

17. Pierce Griffin and W. A. Pullum, "Griffin & Pullum," *Natchez (MS) Daily Courier*, October 15, 1852.

18. David J. Libby, *Slavery and Frontier Mississippi, 1720–1835* (Jackson: University Press of Mississippi, 2004), 65; Gudmestad, *A Troublesome Commerce*, 25.

19. Pierce Griffin and W. A. Pullum, "Fresh Arrival of Negroes," *Mississippi Free Trader*, November 11, 1857.

20. Pierce Griffin and W. A. Pullum, "Fresh Arrival of Negroes," *Mississippi Free Trader*, November 27, 1857; Pierce Griffin and W. A. Pullum, "Fresh Arrival of Negroes," *Mississippi Free Trader*, December 16, 1857; Pierce Griffin and W. A. Pullum, "Fresh Arrival of Negroes," *Natchez (MS) Bulletin*, January 8, 1858; Pierce Griffin and

W. A. Pullum, "Fresh Arrival of Negroes," *Mississippi Free Trader*, January 20, 1858; Pierce Griffin and W. A. Pullum, "Fresh Arrival of Negroes," *Mississippi Free Trader*, March 15, 1858; Pierce Griffin and W. A. Pullum, "Fresh Arrival of Negroes," *Mississippi Free Trader*, March 21, 1859; Pierce Griffin and W. A. Pullum, "Fresh Arrival of Negroes," *Mississippi Free Trader*, April 18, 1859; Pierce Griffin and W. A. Pullum, "Fresh Arrival of Negroes," *Mississippi Free Trader*, May 9, 1859; Pierce Griffin and W. A. Pullum, "Fresh Arrival of Negroes," *Mississippi Free Trader*, May 16, 1859; "Slaves! Slaves!! Slaves!!!," Natchez *Weekly Democrat*, December 29, 1858.

21. Williams v. Talbot, No. 4268, Louisiana Supreme Court, May 1857. *Williams v. Talbot*, No. 7169, was first tried in the Second District Court of New Orleans beginning in December 1853; however, archivists at the New Orleans Public Library's Louisiana Division, City Archives and Special Collections in New Orleans, Louisiana, were unable to locate the original records from the Second District Court suit. Fortunately, records from the lawsuit in the lower court were transcribed in their entirety when the verdict was appealed before the Louisiana Supreme Court. Records from the appeal have been preserved and digitized by the Earl K. Long Library at the University of New Orleans.

22. I am not the first historian to use redhibition suits that centered on enslaved people to learn about the past. Judith Kelleher Schafer's meticulous analysis of Louisiana Supreme Court appeals set the stage for other scholars of antebellum slavery to use these records to write histories of slavery, capitalism, the law, and enslaved people. Schafer, "'Guaranteed Against the Vices and Maladies Prescribed by Law'"; Schafer, *Slavery, the Civil Law, and the Supreme Court of Louisiana*; Gross, *Double Character*; Johnson, *Soul by Soul*.

23. When notaries did this mortgage check, they usually did so in the parish or county where the seller resided. In instances when the seller resided outside of Orleans Parish, sellers sometimes retrieved a certificate of mortgages from their home parish or county and presented it to a New Orleans notary themselves. Only buyers could dispense with the mortgage check, but even they could only do so in writing.

24. For more on New Orleans's notarial archives, see the following: Freudenberger and Pritchett, "Domestic United States Slave Trade"; Sally K. Reeves, "The Plan Book Drawings of New Orleans Notarial Archives: Legal Background and Artistic Development" (paper presented at the semiannual meeting of the American Antiquarian Society at The Arsenal, New Orleans, April 22, 1995); Sally K. Reeves, "Cruising Contractual Waters: Searching for Laffite in the Records of the New Orleans Notarial Archives," *Provenance* 16, no. 1 (January 1998): 1–21.

25. Vance v. Brown, No. 4883, First District Court of Louisiana, New Orleans, September 1822.

26. Solomon Northup, *Twelve Years a Slave: Narrative of Solomon Northup, A Citizen of New-York, Kidnapped in Washington City in 1841, and Rescued in 1853, from a Cotton Plantation Near the Red River, in Louisiana* (Auburn, NY: Derby and Miller, 1853), 78–80.

27. In the Orleans Parish Court, between 1813 and 1846, 109 dissatisfied buyers sued sellers for redhibition on the grounds that the enslaved person they purchased was in the habit of running away. Fifty-eight of these plaintiffs accused their corresponding defendants of withholding that information before the sale. While sellers played an

active, important role in withholding certain information about the people they sold, so did the enslaved individuals themselves.

28. I have located three redhibition suits that centered on enslaved people wherein a buyer sued a seller because the buyer later discovered that the person purchased was not the age that had been relayed to the buyer during a sale or in a contract. For instance, on April 1, 1841, Jean Baptiste Victor Delamoumere sued George Ann Botts for redhibition in the Orleans Parish Court. The contract Jean Baptiste and George signed states that "Fanny is about 30 years of age and a cook." According to his petition, before the sale, Jean Baptiste "discovered that she was a great deal older than said to be, and totally different in those qualities set forth in said act of sale and which induced your petitioner to buy said Fanny." One of the reasons Jean Baptiste filed suit—or at least one of the reasons he thought might compel a New Orleans judge to decide in his favor—was that Fanny was older than he believed she was when he purchased her. Plaintiffs in *Zacharie v. Harvey* (1822) and *Pooley v. Baldwin* (1826) advanced similar claims regarding age. Lamoriniere v. Botts, No. 13809, Orleans Parish Court, New Orleans, April 1841; Zacharie v. Harvey, No. 3149, Orleans Parish Court, New Orleans, April 1822; Pooley v. Baldwin, No. 4377, Orleans Parish Court, New Orleans, March 1824. For more on the relationship between an enslaved person's age and an enslaver's appraisal, see Berry, *The Price for their Pound of Flesh*.

29. When Thomas Boudar testified on his own behalf in *Layson v. Boudar* (1845), he stated that, in regard to one of the eight enslaved men sold to Robert Layson on June 4, 1844, Boudar recalled a previous buyer "disliking a scar which the slave had on his breast and stating that he would not have bought the slave had he seen the scar." While Boudar would not necessarily been inclined to tell whole truths in his defense, he would certainly have been interested in communicating believable lies. Claiming that another buyer returned the enslaved person in question because of a scar would probably have seemed possible to enslavers in the United States by the mid-nineteenth century. For more on testimony and deception, see Johnson, "Inconsistency, Contradiction, and Complete Confusion"; Johnson, *Soul by Soul*; Rogers, *They Were Her Property*; Layson v. Boudar, No. 16714, Orleans Parish Court, New Orleans, June 1845. In *Twelve Years a Slave*, Solomon Northup wrote, "Scars upon a slave's back were considered evidence of a rebellious or unruly spirit, and hurt his sale." Northup, *Twelve Years a Slave*, 80.

30. Riggin v. Kendig, No. 9118, Fourth District Court of New Orleans, New Orleans, August 1855.

31. Riggin v. Kendig, No. 9118, Fourth District Court of New Orleans, New Orleans, August 1855.

32. Johnson, *Wicked Flesh*, 134.

33. The figures in this paragraph are taken from my analysis of New Orleans notary James Graham's contracts between January 1, 1857 and December 31, 1858. James Graham, Notary, Volume 12, January–March 1857, New Orleans, Acts 2569–2766; James Graham; Notary, Volume 13, April–July 1857, New Orleans, Acts 2767–3014; James Graham, Notary, Volume 14, August–December 1857, New Orleans, Acts 3015–3174; James Graham, Notary, Volume 15, January–May 1858, New Orleans, Acts 3175–3441; James Graham, Notary, Volume 16, June–December 1858, New Orleans, Acts 3442–3669.

34. Castillanos v. Pillon, No. 3593, Orleans Parish Court, New Orleans, May 1823.

35. Thomas Henderson, who worked as a cotton factor, testified on Thomas Gatlin's behalf in *Gatlin v. Kendig* (1859). Because Henderson testified that he was then working as Thomas Gatlin's agent, I have surmised that Thomas was probably in the business of growing cotton. *Cohen's New Orleans Directory Including Jefferson City, Gretna, Carrollton, Algiers, and McDonogh* (New Orleans: Office of the Picayune, 1855), 272.

36. *Daily Picayune* (New Orleans), February 6, 1858, Page 8.

37. Joseph A. Beard's office was located at 3 Banks's Arcade and 3 Magazine Street. J. A. Beard & Co., "One Hundred and Fifty Negroes for Sale," *Daily Picayune* (New Orleans), December 20, 1857, p. 5.

38. C. F. Hatcher, "Slave Depot," *Daily Picayune* (New Orleans), February 2, 1858.

39. L. M. Mills, who experienced being sold at an auction in St. Louis, Missouri, in 1847, later described the invasive physical assessments enslavers subjected the enslaved to in the space of the marketplace: "They opened our mouths and looked at our teeth, just as a horse buyer does. When a negro was put on the block he had to help sell himself by telling what he could do. If he refused to praise himself and acted sullen, he was sure to be stripped and given thirty lashes. Frequently a man was compelled to exaggerate his accomplishments, and when his buyer found he could not do what he said he could he would be beaten unmercifully. It was pretty sure to be a thrashing either way." John W. Blassingame, ed., *Slave Testimony: Two Centuries of Letters, Speeches, Interviews, and Autobiographies* (Baton Rouge: Louisiana University Press, 1977), 503.

40. Solomon Northup would later recall the process through which enslavers examined him and those around him. Theophilus Freeman "would make us hold up our heads, walk briskly back and forth, while customers would feel of our hands and arms and bodies, turn us about, ask us what we could do, make us open our mouths and show our teeth." Northup, *Twelve Years a Slave*, 79–80.

41. Northup, *Twelve Years a Slave*, 80.

42. John Brown recalled working to gather information about a man who decided to purchase him. "How I watched them whilst they were driving this bargain! and how I speculated upon the kind of man he was who sought to buy me!" John Brown, *Slave Life in Georgia: A Narrative of the Life, Sufferings, and Escape of John Brown, a Fugitive Slave, now in England*, ed. L. A. Chamerovzow (London: W. M. Watts, 1855), 13–14.

43. Northup, *Twelve Years a Slave*, 80.

44. In *Reckoning with Slavery*, Jennifer L. Morgan interrogates the relationship between the commodification of enslaved people claimed as property and kinship. My analysis demonstrates that by the nineteenth century, enslavers were still deliberately selectively documenting kinship ties among the enslaved. Morgan, *Reckoning with Slavery*.

45. L. Moreau Lislet, *A General Digest of the Acts of the Legislature or Louisiana: Published from the Year 1804, to 1827, Inclusive, and in Force at this last Period, with an Appendix and General Index*, vol. 1 (New Orleans: Benjamin Levy, 1828), 100–119.

46. I have been able to find 10 redhibition suits involving enslaved people that were tried in New Orleans between 1840 and 1860 in which Bernard Kendig was a named defendant, but it is entirely possible that there are other redhibition suits he was involved in that I have yet to discover. If the local dispute was later appealed before the Louisiana Supreme Court, I have listed the citation for the appeal as well. If a citation for a local court dispute is followed by an asterisk (*), it is because I have examined the

records from the appeal but not the original local court records listed in the citation. If the original court records are missing, I have made a note of it along with the date I requested the original records from the New Orleans Public Library, City Archives and Special Collections. In chronological order, by date the plaintiff filed suit, redhibition suits in which Bernard Kendig was a named defendant are as follows: Voorhees v. Dubois and Kendig, No. 13130, Orleans Parish Court, New Orleans, July 1840; Gay v. Kendig, No. 8939, City Court of New Orleans, New Orleans, June 1841*; Gay v. Kendig, No. 4804, Louisiana Supreme Court, June 1842; Riggin v. Kendig, No. 9118, Fourth District Court of New Orleans, New Orleans, August 1855; Riggin v. Kendig, No. 4718, Louisiana Supreme Court, June 1857; Buie v. Kendig, No. 5483, Sixth District Court of New Orleans, New Orleans, August 1857* (requested by the author on August 21, 2017; record is missing); Buie v. Kendig, No. 6356, Louisiana Supreme Court, June 1860; Singleton v. Kendig, No. 11920, Fifth District Court of New Orleans, New Orleans, October 1857; Palmes v. Kendig, No. 11899, Fourth District Court of New Orleans, New Orleans, December 1857* (requested by the author on August 21, 2017; record is missing); Palmes v. Kendig, No. 6279, Louisiana Supreme Court, April 1859; Morris v. Kendig, No. 12949, Fifth District Court of New Orleans, New Orleans, January 1859*; Morris v. Kendig, No. 6385, Louisiana Supreme Court, June 1860; Cochrane v. Kendig, No. 13377, Fifth District Court of New Orleans, New Orleans, January 1860; Belknap v. Kendig, No. 14786, Second District Court of New Orleans, New Orleans, November 1858*; Belknap v. Kendig, No. 6199, Louisiana Supreme Court, April 1860; Gatlin v. Kendig, Fourth District Court of New Orleans, New Orleans, March 1860; Gatlin v. Kendig, No. 6894, Louisiana Supreme Court, November 1860.

47. I have often wondered where Jim Gall was running. It is possible that Mexico could have been his hoped-for destination. For more on enslaved people who escaped to Mexico, see Alice L. Baumgartner, *South to Freedom: Runaway Slaves to Mexico and the Road to the Civil War* (New York: Basic Books, 2020).

48. "Soundness," explains Sharla M. Fett, "in its most basic sense concerned the health of a slave. Yet the definition of soundness included not only the present health of the individual but past and future health as well." *Soundness* was a term used to describe an enslaved person's "capacity to labor, reproduce, obey, and submit." Sharla M. Fett, *Working Cures: Healing, Health, and Power on Southern Slave Plantations* (Chapel Hill: University of North Carolina Press, 2002), 20.

49. While I believe that Dick was in fact ill, there are plenty of reasons to suspect that James Riggin's version of how Dick became sick were not entirely true. In all likelihood, Riggin's attorney helped him fashion Jim's escape and illness into a version that would help him establish cause for redhibition in court. By arguing that Dick's health deteriorated while he was not in Riggin's possession, Riggin's attorney was attempting to preemptively undermine Bernard Kendig and his attorney's defense. According to Louisiana's Civil Code, "the redhibitory action may be commenced after the loss of the object sold, if that loss was not occasioned by the fault of the purchaser." If Kendig and his attorney could argue and demonstrate that Dick was sick due to Riggin's neglect or mistreatment, they could effectively undermine Riggin's attempt to establish cause for redhibition. Louisiana Civil Code of 1825, Section 1, Article 2515, p. 336.

50. John Brown made his escape in 1847, soon after he was sold in New Orleans. Brown, *A Narrative*, 124, 126, 249.

51. John Brown recalled paying attention to his surroundings and working to gather new information: "I was, nevertheless, always on the look-out for a fair chance of escaping and treasured up in my memory such scraps of information as I could draw out of the people that came to the plantation; especially the new hands." Brown, *A Narrative*, 70.

2. Isaac Wright

1. Lawrence, Curator of McMahon v. Botts, No. 13808, Orleans Parish Court, New Orleans, April 1841.

2. This chapter expands the notion of what kinds of labor enslavers demanded of enslaved people. For more on the different kinds of labor enslavers expected from the people they enslaved, see the following: Jennifer L. Morgan, *Laboring Women: Reproduction and Gender in New World Slavery* (Philadelphia: University of Pennsylvania Press, 2004); Jones-Rogers, *They Were Her Property*; Berry, *Price for their Pound of Flesh*; Finley, *Intimate Economy*; Owens, *Consent in the Presence of Force*, 2023.

3. In "Social Death and Political Life in the Study of Slavery," Vincent Brown argues, "the activities of slaves could be more easily understood as having been compelled by the very conditions that slaves have been described as resisting. This would imply a politics of survival, existential struggle transcending resistance against enslavement." Vincent Brown, "Social Death and Political Life in the Study of Slavery," *American Historical Review* 114 (December 2009): 1231–1249, 1246.

4. For more on how enslaved people valued stories about themselves and their respective pasts, see Edward E. Baptist, "'Stol' and Fetched Here': Enslaved Migration, Ex-slave Narratives, and Vernacular History," in *New Studies in the History of American Slavery*, ed. Edward E. Baptist and Stephanie M. H. Camp (Athens: University of Georgia Press, 2006), 243–274.

5. Robert Gudmestad, *Steamboats and the Rise of the Cotton Kingdom* (Baton Rouge: Louisiana State University Press, 2011), 41.

6. Information about Isaac Wright's childhood and work experience come from Wright's testimony and that of his mother, Fanny Douglass. Lawrence, Curator of McMahon v. Botts, No. 13808, Orleans Parish Court, New Orleans, April 1841.

7. For more on the arrests of free people of color in antebellum New Orleans, see John K. Bardes, "Mass Incarceration in the Age of Slavery and Emancipation: Fugitive Slaves, Poor Whites, and Prison Development in Louisiana, 1805–1877" (PhD diss., Tulane University, 2020), 166.

8. The kidnapping and enslavement of Isaac Wright, Stephen Dickenson Jr., and Robert Garrison were not unique. For more on the dangers of kidnapping that free people of color faced, see the following: Carol Wilson, *Freedom at Risk: The Kidnapping of Free Blacks in America, 1780–1865* (Lexington: University Press of Kentucky, 1994); Edlie L. Wong, *Neither Fugitive nor Free: Atlantic Slavery, Freedom Suits, and the Legal Culture of Travel* (New York: New York University Press, 2009); David Fiske, *Solomon Northup's Kindred: The Kidnapping of Free Citizens Before the Civil War* (Santa Barbara, CA: Praeger, 2016); Jonathan Daniel Wells, *The Kidnapping Club:*

Wall Street, Slavery, and Resistance on the Eve of the Civil War (New York: Bold Type Books, 2020).

9. These statements and directions are derived from Isaac Wright's testimony. Lawrence, Curator of McMahon v. Botts, No. 13808, Orleans Parish Court, New Orleans, April 1841.

10. Quotations in this paragraph come from Richard Percival's testimony in *Lawrence, Curator of McMahon v. Botts*. Percival was deposed in Hardin County, Kentucky, on October 9, 1841.

11. For more on deception in the slave market, see Johnson, *Soul by Soul*, 12.

12. This reflects Richard Percival's testimony regarding the story Stephen Dickenson Jr. told about himself and the past. Lawrence, Curator of McMahon v. Botts, No. 13808, Orleans Parish Court, New Orleans, April 1841.

13. According to Stephen Dickenson Jr.'s narrative, "one of these strangers"—one of the two other enslaved people George Ann Botts sent with Isaac Wright, Stephen Dickenson Jr., and Robert Garrison to Vicksburg—"said he was free." A letter that Botts wrote to John Rudisill, his agent in Vicksburg, tells us that he called these two strangers "Sam and Aaron." Stephen Dickenson Jr., "Narrative of Stephen Dickenson, Jr.," *National Anti-Slavery Standard* (New York), October 8, 1840. Lawrence, Curator of McMahon v. Botts, No. 13808, Orleans Parish Court, New Orleans, April 1841.

14. In 1838, John Rudisill identified himself as an auctioneer in various advertisements he had published in Vicksburg, Mississippi, newspapers. J. Rudisill, "Come and buy without Money," *Register* (Vicksburg, MS), March 10, 1838; J. Rudisill, "A Splendid House and Lot at Auction," *Register* (Vicksburg, MS), March 17, 1838; John Rudisill, "NINE LIKELY NEGROES AT AUCTION," *Mississippi Free Trader*, March 17, 1838; J. Rudisill, "Extensive sale of Valuable Property at Public Auction," *Register* (Vicksburg, MS), May 24, 1838; J. Rudisill, "FOR SALE," *Register* (Vicksburg, MS), June 11, 1838.

15. Here, I draw on Stephanie M. H. Camp's concept of rival geographies. According to Camp, "side by side, public and hidden worlds coexisted in the plantation South; their black and white inhabitants shared space, agreed on its importance, and clashed over its uses." I believe the same applies to history, as enslavers and enslaved people shared the past, agreed on its importance, and clashed over its uses. While much of this book is about enslavers' investment in reconstructing and controlling the past, I believe we must also acknowledge that enslaved people valued and used the past in ways that rivaled that of their enslavers. Stephanie M. H. Camp, *Closer to Freedom: Enslaved Women and Everyday Resistance in the Plantation South* (Chapel Hill: University of North Carolina Press, 2004), 2.

16. This reflects Richard Percival's testimony regarding the story Stephen Dickenson Jr. told about himself and the past. Lawrence, Curator of McMahon v. Botts, No. 13808, Orleans Parish Court, New Orleans, April 1841.

17. Quotations in this paragraph come from Stephen Dickenson Jr.'s narrative. Stephen Dickenson Jr., "Narrative of Stephen Dickenson, Jr.," *National Anti-Slavery Standard* (New York), October 8, 1840.

18. In his testimony, Isaac Wright stated the following regarding his discussion with John McMahon: "McMahon asked me 'what I was going to do with the paper and ink.' I told him I was going to write a letter, he asked me, to whom, I said to my friends and

mother in Philadelphia. he asked me if I was ever in Philadelphia. I told him I was. he asked me if I was free, I told him I was." Lawrence, Curator of McMahon v. Botts, No. 13808, Orleans Parish Court, New Orleans, April 1841.

19. Lawrence, Curator of McMahon v. Botts, No. 13808, Orleans Parish Court, New Orleans, April 1841.

20. Quotations in this paragraph come from Isaac Wright's testimony in *Lawrence, Curator of McMahon v. Botts.* Lawrence, Curator of McMahon v. Botts, no. 13808, Orleans Parish Court, New Orleans, April 1841.

21. "The Vigilance Committee," *National Anti-Slavery Standard* (New York), August 27, 1840.

22. James Bradley, "Brief Account of an Emancipated Slave," *Herald of Freedom*, March 7, 1835, 4.

3. Jack Smith

1. Williams v. Talbot, No. 4628, Louisiana Supreme Court, May 1857. *Williams v. Talbot*, No. 7169, was first tried in the Second District Court of New Orleans beginning in December 1853; however, archivists at the New Orleans Public Library's Louisiana Division, City Archives and Special Collections in New Orleans, Louisiana, were unable to locate the original records from the Second District Court suit. Fortunately, records from the lawsuit in the lower court were transcribed in their entirety when the verdict was appealed before the Louisiana Supreme Court. Records from the appeal have been preserved by the Earl K. Long Library at the University of New Orleans.

2. The burden of proof in slave-centered redhibition suits varied based on when the buyer discovered the vice in question, when the buyer filed suit, and the vice or defect at the center of the plaintiff's claim. The nature of a plaintiff's claim as well as when the buyer discovered the vice in question and filed suit also helped define what the plaintiff had to demonstrate in order to establish cause for redhibition. According to Article 2508 of the Louisiana Civil Code, "The buyer who institutes the redhibitory action, must prove that the vice existed before the sale was made to him"; however, "if the vice has made its appearance within three days immediately following the sale, it is presumed to have existed before the sale." The article was amended in 1834 to include specific time constraints for redhibitory vices that were specific to enslaved property. After 1834, buyers who sued for redhibition on the ground that the enslaved person they purchased was a thief or was in the habit of running away did not have to prove that the vice existed before they made their purchase *if* they discovered the vice within two months of the date of sale; additionally, if a buyer discovered any "bodily or mental maladies" within 15 days of the sale and sued for redhibition, the court would presume that the vice existed before the sale. There were thus instances when the burden of proof was such that a plaintiff could rely on an act of sale and the plaintiff's own assessment of an enslaved person's diminished value and utility to sue for redhibition. That was not the case in *Williams v. Talbot* (1853). The amendments to Article 2508 did not apply to enslaved people who had been in Louisiana for more than eight months. They would also not apply when "unusual punishments have been inflicted" on the enslaved person in question. Louisiana Civil Code of 1825, Book III, Title VII, Chapter I, Section III, Article 2508.

3. Not every redhibition suit tried before the Orleans Parish Court centered on just one enslaved person. Sometimes groups of enslaved people or mothers and their children found themselves at the center of the same lawsuit. Additionally, being led into court was not the only way that enslaved people who found themselves at the center of redhibition suits were exploited as evidence. Some were subject to invasive physical examinations so that physicians could gather evidence from their bodies, while others, who had passed away, were subject to postmortem examinations. Even in death, enslaved people could be mined for evidence that would fill the pockets of those who enslaved them in life.

4. While other redhibition suits involved out-of-state witnesses, *Williams v. Talbot* (1853) is the only redhibition suit that I have been able to find in which the enslaved person at the center of the dispute was taken out of state so that he or she could be present while a witness was deposed. I examined each of the extant 17,006 civil suits tried before the Orleans Parish Court between 1813 and 1846—the years of the court's existence—to locate each of the 295 slave-centered redhibition suits tried before the court.

5. Marisa J. Fuentes, "Enslaved People Were Not Meant to Be Historicized" (presented at "Slavery and the University—Research in Action" panel, American Historical Association, 132nd Annual Meeting, Washington, DC, January 4, 2018).

6. George Davis testified in *Williams v. Talbot* (1853) on April 13, 1854. Davis claimed that he "had a large dealings with the plaintiff on the first of January 1853," when the "plaintiff purchased slaves from witness and defendant." While he did not discuss the terms of his and Williams's agreement, we can gather some information about the terms of the sale from his testimony—namely, that it involved a 60-day warranty: "he [Williams] had the privilege of returning any of the negroes he purchased from me within sixty days." Williams v. Talbot, No. 4628, Louisiana Supreme Court, May 1857.

7. In 1852, William F. Talbot published at least two advertisements in New Orleans newspapers for enslaved people he was attempting to sell. Both advertisements list the address of his "old stand" as no. 7 Moreau Street, New Orleans. "NEGROES just arrived," *Daily Delta* (New Orleans), March 3, 1852; "Slaves–Slaves," *Daily Picayune* (New Orleans), April 4, 1852.

8. Quotations in this paragraph come from George Davis's testimony in *Williams v. Talbot* (1857). Williams v. Talbot, No. 4628, Louisiana Supreme Court, May 1857.

9. For more on what these appraisals looked like, see Johnson, *Soul by Soul*, 162–188; Jones-Rogers, *They Were Her Property*, 81–100.

10. According to testimony from *Williams v. Talbot* (1853), Nathan Harroldson sold Jack Smith to Jacob Hall in Jackson County, Missouri, in the spring of 1852 for $800; Hall then sold Jack Smith to Jabez Smith in Missouri in either November or late October for $900; Jabez Smith then sold Jack Smith to John Mattingly in November; sometime between November and January 1, 1853, Jack Smith was transported to New Orleans and purchased by William F. Talbot. Williams v. Talbot, No. 4628, Louisiana Supreme Court, May 1857.

11. Testimony from *Williams v. Talbot* (1853) places Jack Smith in Independence, Missouri—located in the northwestern part of the state in Jackson County—in 1845 or 1846 at the earliest. Later in the chapter, I will explain why I believe this timeline to be accurate.

12. Harrison Anthony Trexler, "Slavery in Missouri" (PhD diss., Johns Hopkins University, 1914), 13.

13. John Mattingly published advertisements in southern newspapers during the 1840s and 1850s, wherein he expressed his wish to purchase large numbers of enslaved people. In some of these advertisements, Mattingly disclosed that he wished to purchase enslaved people "expressly for the Louisiana and Mississippi market." "Slaves–Slaves," *Daily Missouri Republican* (St. Louis), September 18, 1856.

14. According to the testimony of Jacob Hall, "Mattingly bought said slave [Jack Smith] for a southern market." Williams v. Talbot, No. 4268, Louisiana Supreme Court, May 1857.

15. John Mattingly published the same advertisements in the following issues of the *Louisville Daily Journal*: "100 Negroes Wanted," *Louisville (KY) Daily Journal*, December 12, 13, 18, 25, 27.

16. Additionally, an advertisement from 1849 lists John Mattingly as the agent of three traders, "Hunter, Murphy, and Talbott." I believe the "Talbott" listed in the advertisement is likely William F. Talbot. "300 REWARD," *Louisville (KY) Daily Journal*, December 22, 1849.

17. William F. Talbot's advertisement first appeared in the *Daily Picayune* (New Orleans) on September 30, 1852. He continued running the ad the following year. "150 Negroes for Sale," *Daily Picayune* (New Orleans), September 30, 1852.

18. George Davis testified as follows: "Plaintiff purchased slaves from witness and Defendant. About thirty or forty days after the purchase of the slaves from Defendant, one of the slaves was returned to defendant for a defect of sight, and Talbot returned the money with the expense of bring him down." Williams v. Talbot, No. 4628, Louisiana Supreme Court, May 1857.

19. Alfred A. Williams's letter to William F. Talbot was used as evidence in *Williams v. Talbot* (1853). Williams v. Talbot, No. 4628, Louisiana Supreme Court, May 1857.

20. Williams v. Talbot, No. 4628, Louisiana Supreme Court, May 1857.

21. Keys v. Brown, No. 7718, Orleans Parish Court, September 1834; Devergies v. Chabert, No. 6115, Orleans Parish Court, November 1831; Layson v. Boudar, No. 16714, Orleans Parish Court, June 1845.

22. Lewis Sharp and Sally Handley Fisher—the wife of one of Jack Smith's previous owners and the daughter of America Palmer—were mentioned in A. J. Villere's letter but did not testify in *Williams v. Talbot* (1853).

23. Williams v. Talbot, No. 4628, Louisiana Supreme Court, May 1857.

24. Williams v. Talbot, No. 4628, Louisiana Supreme Court, May 1857.

25. *Seventh Census of the United States 1850*, Parish of West Baton Rouge, Louisiana, Roll M432–229, p. 254B, image 494, Alfred A. Williams; *Seventh Census of the United States 1850, Slave Schedules*, Schedule II, Parish of West Baton Rouge, Louisiana, Alfred A. Williams; *Seventh Census of the United States 1850, Slave Schedules*, Schedule II, 8th Ward, Parish of East Baton Rouge, Louisiana, Alfred A. Williams. The following is taken from Joseph Karl Menn's work on East Baton Rouge slaveholders: "It is extremely difficult at times to be certain whether a person holding slaves in one parish was the same person holding slaves in another. If the name of the slaveholder was given in exactly the same

form in two or more parishes, and if he is found on Schedule No. 1 in only one parish, or perhaps in no parish, then it may be assumed with a fair amount of certainty that the two or more holdings in two or more parishes belonged to the same person. . . . The large holdings of A. A. Williams, Alfred Williams, and Alfred A. Williams pose a unique problem. If these holdings all belonged to the same individual, Williams was one of the very largest of Louisiana slaveholders." Joseph Karl Menn, *The Large Slaveholders of East Baton Rouge, Louisiana–1860* (Pelican Publishing, 1998), 102–103.

26. Alfred Williams was in Cuba with his family between January and February 1853. According to George Davis—a New Orleans slave trader who also sold enslaved people to Williams on January 1, 1853, and who testified in *Williams v. Talbot* (1853)—while Williams was out of town, his father-in-law, Nolan Stewart, returned one of the enslaved men Williams had purchased from Davis because of a "defect of sight." The incident illuminates another individual whom Williams likely trusted to manage and make decisions about the people he claimed as his enslaved property.

27. Bagasse were dried cane husks that were used to fuel furnaces on sugar plantations. Enslaved people on these plantations produced sugar in open kettles over furnaces. For more on sugar production in the antebellum Louisiana, see Richard Follett, *The Sugar Masters: Planters and Slaves in Louisiana's Cane World, 1820–1860* (Baton Rouge: Louisiana State University Press, 2005), 32–38.

28. Quotations in this paragraph are taken from William F. J. Davis's testimony. When he testified, he was still employed on Alfred A. Williams's plantation. Williams v. Talbot, No. 4628, Louisiana Supreme Court, May 1857.

29. For more on overseers and management strategies, see the following: Johnson, *River of Dark Dreams*, 166–171; Tristan Stubbs, *Masters of Violence: The Plantation Overseers of Eighteenth-Century Virginia, South Carolina, and Georgia* (Columbia: University of South Carolina Press 2018); William E. Wiethoff, *Crafting the Overseer's Image* (Columbia: University of South Carolina Press, 2006), 3–31; Baptist, *Half Has Never Been Told*, 114–121; Rosenthal, *Accounting for Slavery*, 27–29; Follett, *Sugar Masters*, 91–113, 173–179.

30. Frederick Douglass, *Narrative of the Life of Frederick Douglass, an American Slave: Written by Himself* (Boston: Anti-Slavery Office, 1845), 20–22.

31. Follett, *Sugar Masters*, 11–12.

32. My assertion that Dr. Favrot examined Jack Smith twice is indicative of my decision to believe Dr. Favrot's version of when and how often he examined Jack Smith, which contradicts William F. J. Davis's testimony. Davis, Alfred Williams's overseer, claimed that Dr. Favrot "was first called to see him [Smith] in the month of July or August 1853," but Dr. Favrot testified he examined Jack Smith only twice—the first time in October and the second in November 1853. I have concluded that Davis was likely lying in an attempt to demonstrate that his employer had ensured—far earlier than he actually did—that Jack Smith was promptly treated for his illness.

33. Quotations in this paragraph come from Dr. Louis Favrot's testimony in *Williams v. Talbot* (1853). Williams v. Talbot, No. 4628, Louisiana Supreme Court, May 1857.

34. Depending on physicians to historicize an illness did not always work, as judges and juries were not always convinced such an assessment was possible or plausible.

Additionally—though this was not the case in *Williams v. Talbot* (1853)—in cases when the enslaved person at the center of the dispute had died, plaintiffs sometimes had physicians perform autopsies and discuss their findings on the stand. Even in death, slaveowners examined and dissected enslaved people's bodies for valuable information.

35. *Soundness* was a term used to identify an enslaved person's "capacity to labor, reproduce, obey, and submit." Fett, *Working Cures: Healing, Health, and Power on Southern Slave Plantations* (Chapel Hill: University of North Carolina Press), 20.

36. James Wallace testified on Alfred A. Williams's behalf in the Sixth District Court of Louisiana in West Baton Rouge Parish on August 14, 1854. Williams v. Talbot, No. 4628, Louisiana Supreme Court, May 1857.

37. I have written *probably* here because while Wallace testified that he and Jack Smith left from New Orleans on board the *Peter Tellon*, he did not give the exact date. Judging from newspaper advertisements and articles describing the steamboat's journey in April 1854 as well as when Wallace stated they arrived in Independence, I have reasoned that they were probably aboard the *Peter Tellon* when it departed on April 18, 1854. "Steamboat Departures To Day," *Daily Picayune* (New Orleans), April 18, 1854, p. 2.

38. The following newspaper articles describe the *Peter Tellon* and its regular journeys up and down the Mississippi River: "Steamboat Departures Today," *Daily Picayune* (New Orleans), April 18, 1854; "Receipts of Produce," *Daily Picayune* (New Orleans), March 17, 1854; "Marine Intelligence," *Daily Picayune* (New Orleans), April 14, 1854; "Steamboats Built in the District of Louisville during the Year 1853," *Crescent* (New Orleans), January 11, 1854; "Memorandum," *Louisville (KY) Daily Courier*, April 19, 1854; "The river yesterday . . . ," *Louisville (KY) Daily Courier*, January 23, 1854; "Sickness on the River," *Louisville (KY) Daily Courier*, January 23, 1854.

39. When James Wallace testified in the Sixth District Court of Louisiana in West Baton Rouge Parish on August 14, 1854, he claimed that during his and Jack Smith's journey to Independence, Missouri, he ensured that Smith was not "exposed to the cold or wet." I believe that this is one instance in which Wallace lied to help his employer win his lawsuit. Wallace and even Alfred Williams were in an awkward position when it came to this journey. To establish cause for redhibition, Robert Hardin Marr had to argue not only that Jack Smith was sick and useless but also that Williams had not contributed to Smith's deteriorating health. Exposing an enslaved person to the cold and wet during an extensive journey to Missouri and back would have almost certainly been interpreted by the Louisiana court as evidence of Williams's having contributed to Smith's illness. Wallace, as a man in Williams's employ, thus had sufficient reason to exaggerate and even lie about this particular point. The following sources go into detail regarding the physical dimensions of steamboats not unlike the *Peter Tellon* and the steamboat world as it then was and helped me to reach this conclusion: Kevin Crisman, William B. Less, and John Davis, "The Western River Steamboat *Heroine*, 1832–1838, Oklahoma USA: Excavations, Summary of Findings, and History," *International Journal of Nautical Archaeology* 42, no. 2 (June 2013): 365–381; Kevin J. Crisman, "The Western River Steamboat *Heroine*, 1832–1838, Oklahoma USA: Construction," *International Journal of Nautical Archaeology* 43, no. 1 (November 2013): 128–150; John

Harrison Morrison, *History of Steam Navigation* (New York: W. F. Sametz and Co., 1903), 263; Buchanan, *Black Life on the Mississippi*, 61, 66.

40. Neither America Palmer nor Daniel D. White could remember exactly when they met Jack Smith; both testified it was either in the spring of 1845 or 1846.

41. Williams v. Talbot, No. 4628, Louisiana Supreme Court, May 1857.

42. Quotations in this paragraph come from America Palmer's testimony. Williams v. Talbot, No. 4628, Louisiana Supreme Court, May 1857.

43. Freeman McKinney was deposed in San Jose, California, on June 13, 1854. Williams v. Talbot, No. 4628, Louisiana Supreme Court, May 1857.

44. Nathan Harrelson did not testify in *Williams v. Talbot* (1853). O. P. Williams & Co., ed., *The History of Cass and Bates Counties, Missouri: Containing a History of These Counties, Their Cities, Towns, Etc., Etc., Biographical Sketches of Their Citizens, General and Local Statistics, History of Missouri, Map of Cass and Bates Counties, Etc.* (St. Joseph, MO: National Historical Company, 1883), 561–562; Allen Glenn, *History of Cass County, Missouri* (Topeka, KS: Historical Publishing Company, 1917), 320–322; *Seventh Census of the United States, 1850*, Schedule I, Sixteenth District, Cass County, Missouri; *1850 Federal Census, Slave Schedules*, Schedule II, Sixteenth District, Cass County, Missouri, p. 337.

45. Jacob Hall also testified that Jack Smith "never had any sickness" while in his possession, and he believed that he had "never owned a more healthy negro." Robert G. Smart, another farmer and Hall's neighbor, who was also deposed, testified that he frequently saw Jack Smith on Hall's farm, where Smith "worked a great deal . . . almost daily from the time Col. Hall bought him." Although he had never previously examined Smith, Smart testified, he believed that he was a "healthy, stout, and hearty black negro and a good hand to work on the farm." Williams v. Talbot, No. 4628, Louisiana Supreme Court, May 1857. Although Alfred Williams had no way to recoup his investment in Jack Smith from Jacob Hall—Hall had not sold Smith to Williams—in some cases, defendants who lost redhibition suits filed lawsuits against previous sellers to recoup their losses. As a lawyer and a slaveholder, Hall may have considered whether his description of Smith's health could be subsequently used against him. I thus have suspicions of Hall's and Smart's testimony regarding Smith's health. They had no reason, however, to lie about the identity of the person (Nathan Harrelson) from whom Hall had purchased Smith, as such information could not result in Hall's being held liable for Jack Smith's supposed deficiencies; therefore, I have deemed that assertion more likely.

46. Defendants in redhibition suits frequently called in previous sellers to avoid the cost of a canceled sale, whether or not a previous seller had warranted the person in question. Because Palmer and White never owned Smith, there was no way they could have ever been held liable for his deficiencies in court. And as Fisher had passed away and, according to their testimony, had returned Smith at least seven years earlier, no one in Palmer's family could be held liable, either.

47. Giraudeau, f.w.c. v. Tate, No. 6106, Orleans Parish Court, November 1831.

48. When Robert G. Smart testified before an Independence justice of the peace, William L. Bone, on August 25, 1854, he recounted the circumstances surrounding America Palmer's and Daniel D. White's deposition, explaining, "Jack was present at the time."

49. Robert Hardin Marr's second set of questions for the witnesses in Independence, Missouri, are as follows: "Second. Do you know anything of a negro named Jack 'or Jack Smith,' formerly the property of Nathan Harroldson? If you do, State where you saw him first, in whose possession he was, when and where you saw him last, in whose possession he then was, and whether or not you recognize the Jack that you saw last, as the same Jack you saw first."

50. Williams v. Talbot, No. 4628, Louisiana Supreme Court, May 1857.

51. Quotations and information regarding the last months of Jack Smith's life come from J. A. Cassot's testimony. He was deposed before the Sixth District Court of Louisiana in West Baton Rouge Parish on August 17, 1854. Williams v. Talbot, No. 4628, Louisiana Supreme Court, May 1857.

52. For more on the commodification of enslaved people after their demise, see Berry, *Price for Their Pound of Flesh*, 148–193.

53. Williams v. Talbot, No. 4628, Louisiana Supreme Court, May 1857.

4. Transforming Betsey into Rachel

1. Betsey alias Rachel v. St. Amand, No. 2226, Orleans Parish Court, New Orleans, June 1819.

2. John K. Bardes, "Mass Incarceration in the Age of Slavery and Emancipation: Fugitive Slaves, Poor Whites, and Prison Development in Louisiana, 1805–1877" (PhD diss., Tulane University, 2020), 205.

3. Quotations are taken from Betsey's petition. Betsey alias Rachel v. St. Amand, No. 2226, Orleans Parish Court, New Orleans, June 1819.

4. Louisiana Civil Code, Title VI, Chapter 3, Article 177, p. 28.

5. Nicholson, f.w.c. v. Thompson, No. 4783, Orleans Parish Court, New Orleans, August 1827.

6. Tait v. The Mayor, Alderman, and Inhabitants of New Orleans, No. 8539, Orleans Parish Court, New Orleans, November 1835.

7. Erwin v. Hutchinson, No. 2304, First District Court of Louisiana, April 1819.

8. Schafer, *Becoming Free, Remaining Free*, 8.

9. Henry A. Bullard and Thomas Curry, eds., *A New Digest of the Statute Laws of the State of Louisiana from the Change of Government to the Year 1841, Inclusive* (New Orleans: E. Johns and Co., Stationers' Hall, 1842), 46–73.

10. Rachel, f.w.c. v. Simon Knight, No. 2893, Orleans Parish Court, New Orleans, May 1820.

11. Louisa Davis, f.w.c. v. George Shall and Wife and Emphraim Shall and Wife, No. 7198, Orleans Parish Court, New Orleans, January 1834.

12. Peter v. Lamothe, No. 1859, Orleans Parish Court, New Orleans, October 1818.

13. Marie Joseph Meyer, f.w.c. v. Jean Baptiste Camille, f.m.c., No. 12989, Orleans Parish Court, New Orleans, June 1840.

14. Mathias Gilbert, f.m.c. v. John S. Turner, No. 2033, Orleans Parish Court, New Orleans, September 1818.

15. When it came to the social status of free people of color in the Atlantic world, written evidence was an important, essential part of how individuals demonstrated and worked to maintain their freedom. Rebecca J. Scott and Jean M. Hébrard, *Freedom*

Papers: An Atlantic Odyssey in the Age of Emancipation (Cambridge: Harvard University Press, 2012).

16. Gilbert, f.m.c. v. Turner, No. 2033, Orleans Parish Court, New Orleans, September 1818.

17. Howard v. Martin, No. 147, Orleans Parish Court, New Orleans, October 1813; Luchal v. Lamothe, No. 1210, Orleans Parish Court, New Orleans, February 1817; Davis, f.w.c. v. Shall, et al., No. 7198, January 1834; Tait v. The Mayor, Alderman, and Inhabitants of New Orleans, No. 8539, Orleans Parish, New Orleans, November 1835; Meyer, f.w.c. v. Camille, f.m.c., No. 12,997, Orleans Parish, New Orleans, June 1840; Meyer, f.w.c v. Camille, f.m.c., No. 12989, Orleans Parish, New Orleans, June 1840; Coby, f.m.c. v. Miesegas, et al., No. 16954, Orleans Parish, New Orleans, April 1846; Catherine, f.w.c. v. Prival, No. 2129, Orleans Parish, New Orleans, April 1819; Gilbert, f.m.c. v. Turner, No. 2033, Orleans Parish, New Orleans, September 1818; Francois, f.w.c. v. Widow Chancerel, No. 6051, Orleans Parish, New Orleans, August 1831; Nicholson, f.w.c. v. Thompson, No. 4783, Orleans Parish, New Orleans, August 1827; Betsy alias Rachel v. St. Amand, No. 2226, Orleans Parish, New Orleans, June 1819; Jackson v. Heirs of Bridges, No. 10632, Orleans Parish, New Orleans, March 1838; Britain v. Dick and McCoy, No. 1836, Orleans Parish, New Orleans, September 1818; Dunbar, f.m.c. v. Layton, No. 4072, Orleans Parish, New Orleans, March 1825; Mariano v. Breedlove, No. 5276, Orleans Parish, New Orleans, May 1829; Genevieve Isabelle alias Labelle f.w.c. v. Dauphin et al., No. 6256, Orleans Parish, New Orleans, February 1833; Toussine, f.w.c. v. Zelia, f.w.c., No. 7524, Orleans Parish, New Orleans, May 1834; Felix, f.m.c. v. Papet, No. 8357, Orleans Parish, New Orleans, June 1835; Bideau v. Charles, f.m.c., No. 13821, Orleans Parish, New Orleans, April 1841.

18. Britain, f.m.c. v. Dick and McCoy, No. 1836, Orleans Parish Court, New Orleans, September 1818.

19. Louisiana Civil Code of 1808, Book III, Title XIX, Chapter I, Article 1.

20. Louisiana Civil Code of 1825, Book III, Title XXII, Chapter 1, Article 3245, p. 422: "Mortgage is a right granted to the creditor over the property of his debtor, for the security of his debt, and gives him the power of having the property seized and sold in default of payment."

21. Louisiana Civil Code of 1808, Book III, Title XIX, Chapter I, Article 4; Louisiana Civil Code of 1825, Book III, Title XXII, Chapter 1, Article 3253, p. 423.

22. Louisiana Civil Code of 1808, Book III, Title XIX, Chapter I, Articles 5, 8, 15; Louisiana Civil Code of 1825, Book III, Title XXII, Chapter 1, Section 1, Article 3257, p. 423; Louisiana Civil Code of 1825, Book III, Title XXII, Chapter 1, Section 2, Article 3279, p. 425; Louisiana Civil Code of 1825, Book III, Title XXII, Chapter 1, Section 3, Article 3289, p. 426.

23. Louisiana Civil Code of 1808, Book III, Title XIX, Chapter I, Articles 5 and 6; Louisiana Civil Code of 1825, Book III, Title XXII, Chapter 1, Section 3, Article 3272, p. 425.

24. Louisiana Civil Code of 1808, Book III, Title XIX, Chapter III, Section 3, Article 52: "Though it is a rule that the conventional mortgage is acquired by the sole consent of the parties, and the judicial and legal mortgages by the judgment or law which grants it, nevertheless, in order to protect the good faith of third persons who

may be ignorant of such covenants and to prevent fraud, law directs that the conventional and judicial mortgages, shall be recorded or entered in a public *folio* book kept for the purpose in the city of New-Orleans for the whole territory."

25. Louisiana Civil Code of 1808, Book III, Title XIX, Chapter III, Section 3, Articles 52 and 55.

26. Louisiana Civil Code of 1825, Book III, Title XXII, Chapter II, Section III, Article 3351, p. 435.

27. Louisiana Civil Code of 1808, Book III, Title XIX, Chapter III, Section III, Article 58; Louisiana Civil Code of 1825, Book III, Title XXII, Chapter II, Section III, Article 3356, p. 436.

28. Neither the original mortgage agreement that Joseph Erwin, Samuel Downey, and John Hutchinson signed nor a transcribed copy of the document was included in court records from *Betsey, alias Rachel, f.w.c. v. St. Amand* (1819). Instead, the recorder of mortgages for Louisiana submitted a certificate of mortgages dated March 18, 1820, wherein he confirmed that he possessed a record of the three men entering into said agreement.

29. Nicholson, f.w.c. v. Thompson, No. 4783, Orleans Parish Court, New Orleans, August 1827.

30. Alice Pemble White, "The Plantation Experience of Joseph and Lavinia Erwin, 1807–1836," *Louisiana Historical Quarterly* 27, no. 2 (April 1944): 353–355, 360, 383; David D. Plater, *The Butlers of Iberville Parish, Louisiana: Dunboyne Plantation in the 1800s* (Baton Rouge: Louisiana State University Press, 2015), 35.

31. Davenport v. Dixon, No. 6040, Orleans Parish Court, New Orleans, July 1831.

5. Sarah Ann Connor

1. Quotations come from Sarah Ann Connor's petition in *Connor v. Freeman* (1846). Connor, f.w.c. v. Freeman, No. 24796, First District Court of Louisiana, New Orleans, April 1846.

2. Connor, f.w.c. v. The Bank of Kentucky, No. 1704, Fourth District Court of New Orleans, New Orleans, April 1848; Connor, f.w.c. v. Dunbar, No. 1193, Fifth District Court of New Orleans, New Orleans, April 1848.

3. "CITY INTELLIGENCE," *Daily Picayune* (New Orleans), August 13, 1851.

4. Trouillot, *Silencing the Past*, 106.

5. Schafer, *Slavery, the Civil Law, and the Supreme Court of Louisiana*, 175; Johnson, *Soul by Soul*, 114.

6. Finley, *Intimate Economy*, 69.

7. Louisiana Civil Code of 1825, Title VI, Chapter III, Article 174, p. 28.

8. Schafer, *Becoming Free, Remaining Free*.

9. Information about Sarah Connor's life in the boardinghouse come from the testimony of Louis Exnicios in Dunbar v. Connor, f.w.c., No. 1700, Louisiana Supreme Court, May 1850.

10. Melissa Garrison testified on Sarah Connor's behalf in Connor, f.w.c. v. The Bank of Kentucky, No. 1704, Fourth District Court of New Orleans, New Orleans, April 1848.

11. Northup, *Twelve Years a Slave*, 75.

12. Connor, f.w.c. v. A.F. Dunbar, No. 1193, Fifth District Court of New Orleans, New Orleans, April 1848; Dunbar v. Connor, f.w.c. and Freeman, No. 1700, Louisiana Supreme Court, May 1849.

13. Bank of Kentucky v. Connor, f.w.c. and Freeman, No. 1428, Fifth District Court of New Orleans, New Orleans, July 1848.

14. For more on Sarah Connor's business, see Finley, *Intimate Economy*.

15. Williams v. Freeman, No. 15702, Orleans Parish Court, New Orleans, March 1843.

16. The concept of "domestic authority" comes from Whitney Nell Stewart, *This is Our Home: Slavery and Struggle on Southern Plantations* (Chapel Hill: University of North Carolina Press, November 2023).

17. There is no record of Sarah Connor discussing the arrests. Samuel Powers's testimony remains the only source of this particular piece of information; although Powers was invested in seeing Connor enslaved, I do not believe that lying about Connor being arrested would have bolstered Powers's case against Sarah in *Connor, f.w.c. v. Powers and Johnson* (1849). I have thus reasoned that in this particular instance, he was likely telling the truth.

18. "The Courts," *Daily Picayune* (New Orleans), March 29, 1851; "Parish Prison," *Crescent* (New Orleans), July 17, 1848, 3.

19. Louisiana Civil Code of 1825, Title VI, Chapter III, Article 189, 32.

20. Petition, Connor, f.w.c. v. The Bank of Kentucky, No. 1704, Fourth District Court of New Orleans, New Orleans, April 1848; Petition, Amis v. The Bank of Kentucky, No. 1794, Fourth District Court of New Orleans, New Orleans, May 1848.

21. Sarah Connor and Junius Amis both hired the attorneys Hunt and Lacy to file their lawsuits against the Bank of Kentucky.

22. Connor, f.w.c. v. The Bank of Kentucky, No. 1704, Fourth District Court of New Orleans, New Orleans, April 1848; Connor, f.w.c. v. Dunbar, No. 1193, Fifth District Court of New Orleans, New Orleans, April 1848; Amis v. The Bank of Kentucky, No. 1794, Fourth District Court of New Orleans, New Orleans, May 1848; Amis v. A. F. Dunbar, et al., No. 1230, Fifth District Court of New Orleans, New Orleans, May 1848.

23. Amis v. The Bank of Kentucky, No. 1794, Fourth District Court of New Orleans, New Orleans, May 1848; Amis v. The Bank of Kentucky, No. 1428, Louisiana Supreme Court, April 1849.

24. Lawsuits that Junius Amis filed and involved Theophilus Freeman are as follows: Amis v. The Bank of Louisiana, No. 21964, First District Court of Louisiana, New Orleans, December 1842; Amis v. Merchants Insurance Company of New Orleans, No. 24127, Fifth District Court of New Orleans, New Orleans, May 1845; Amis v. James, et al., No. 1890, First District Court of Louisiana, New Orleans, February 1848; Amis v. The Bank of Kentucky, No. 1794, Fourth District Court of New Orleans, New Orleans, May 1848; Amis v. Dunbar, Syndic of John Goodin and Co., No. 1230, Fifth District Court of New Orleans, New Orleans, May 1848. The following are lawsuits having to do with Theophilus Freeman in which Junius Amis was involved as neither a plaintiff or defendant: Williams v. Freeman, No. 15702, Orleans Parish Court, New Orleans, March 1843; Petway v. John Goodin and Co., No. 23217, First District Court of Louisiana, New Orleans, April 1844; Lambeth and Thompson v. Freeman, No. 6492,

Commercial Court of New Orleans, New Orleans, February 1844; Stewart v. Sowles and Hite, No. 24766, Fifth District Court of New Orleans, New Orleans, March 1846.

25. Amis v. Merchants Insurance Company of New Orleans, No. 24127, Fifth District Court of New Orleans, New Orleans, May 1845.

26. Connor, f.w.c. v. Dunbar, No. 1193, Fifth District Court of New Orleans, New Orleans, April 1848; Connor, f.w.c. v. The Bank of Kentucky, No. 1704, Fourth District Court of New Orleans, New Orleans, April 1848.

27. Schafer, *Becoming Free, Remaining Free*, 97.

28. Hawkins v. Van Wickle, No. 1501, Louisiana Supreme Court, January 1828.

29. Louisiana Civil Code of 1825, Book 1, Title V, Chapter 1, Articles 137 and 139 include laws relating to concubines and grounds for divorce; Book 1: Of Persons, Title VII, Chapter III of Louisiana's Civil Code discusses concubines and illegitimate children; Book 1: Of Persons, Title IV, Chapter II, Article 95 explicitly prevents "free white persons" from marrying "free persons of color"; Book III: Of the Different Modes of Acquiring Things, Title II, Chapter II, Article 1468 regulates the transfer of money and property between people living in "open concubinage."

30. Louisiana Civil Code of 1825, Book III, Title II, Chapter II, Article 1468, p. 204.

31. Louisiana Civil Code of 1825, Book III, Title VI, Chapter I, Article 2315, p. 313.

32. Louisiana Civil Code of 1825, Book III, Title VI, Chapter I, Articles 2368 and 2361, pp. 318–319.

33. For another example of a nonmarried couple—a free woman of color and a white man, whose relationship was nevertheless subject to legal oversight in antebellum New Orleans—see Owens, *Consent in the Presence of Force*, 104–118.

34. Quoted text taken from Caroline M. Williams's testimony on Sarah Connor's behalf. Williams was deposed in Mississippi. Connor, f.w.c. v. The Bank of Kentucky, No. 1704, Fourth District Court of New Orleans, New Orleans, April 1848.

35. Connor, f.w.c. v. The Bank of Kentucky, No. 1704, Fourth District Court of New Orleans, New Orleans, April 1848.

36. A.F. Dunbar v. Connor, f.w.c., No. 2496, Fifth District Court of New Orleans, New Orleans, May 1849; A. F. Dunbar v. Connor, f.w.c., No. 1700, Louisiana Supreme Court, May 1850.

37. Lunsford, f.w.c. v. Coquillon, No. 815, Louisiana Supreme Court, May 1824.

38. Schafer, *Slavery, the Civil Law, and the Supreme Court of Louisiana*, 263.

39. *Acts Passed at the First Session of the First Legislature of the State of Louisiana. Begun and Held in the City of New Orleans, on the 9th Day of February, 1846* (New Orleans: W. Van Benthuysen and P. Besancon, Jr. State Printers, 1846), 163.

40. Dunbar, et al. v. Connor, f.w.c. and Freeman, No. 2496, Fifth District Court of New Orleans, New Orleans, May 1849; Bank of Kentucky v. Connor, f.w.c. and Freeman, No. 1428, Fifth District Court of New Orleans, New Orleans, July 1848.

41. Dunbar et al. v. Connor, f.w.c. and Freeman, No. 2496, Fifth District Court of New Orleans, New Orleans, May 1849; Bank of Kentucky v. Connor, f.w.c. and Freeman, No. 1428, Fifth District Court of New Orleans, New Orleans, July 1848.

42. Schafer, *Becoming Free, Remaining Free*, 130–144.

43. "CITY INTELLIGENCE. The Case of Sarah Conner," *Daily Picayune* (New Orleans), August 7, 1851.

44. "CITY INTELLIGENCE. Trial for Perjury," *Daily Picayune* (New Orleans), August 9, 1851.

45. I examined the docket book that lists the 1,361 civil suits and criminal trials conducted in the First District Court of Louisiana in 1851. First District Court of Louisiana, General Dockets, vol. II, February 7, 1851–December 24, 1856, New Orleans Public Library, City Archives and Special Collections.

46. "CITY INTELLIGENCE. Trial for Perjury," *Daily Picayune* (New Orleans), March 31, 1852; The State v. Sarah Connor, f.w.c., No. 7158, First District Court of New Orleans, New Orleans, January 1852.

47. The State of Louisiana v. Sarah Connor, f.w.c., No. 2759, Louisiana Supreme Court, June 1852.

48. The following reports from the Louisiana State Penitentiary's board of directors do not include Sarah Connor: *Report of the Board of Directors of the Penitentiary of the State of Louisiana* (New Orleans: Emile La Sere, State Printer, 1853); *Annual Report of the Board of Directors, Clerk, and Officers of the Louisiana Penitentiary, at Baton Rouge: For the Year Ending December 31, 1854* (New Orleans: Emile La Sere, State Printer, 1855); *Annual Report of the Board of Directors of the Louisiana Penitentiary to the Governor of the State of Louisiana, January 1856* (New Orleans: John Claiborne, State Printer, 1856); *Report of the Board of Control of the Louisiana Penitentiary* (Baton Rouge: J. M. Taylor, State Printer, 1859).

49. Connor, f.w.c. v. The Bank of Kentucky, No. 1704, Fourth District Court of New Orleans, New Orleans, April 1848. Judge M. M. Reynolds ordered Sarah Connor "to pay to the Bank of Kentucky 8% interest from 27th May 1848 until 22 May 1854 on the sum of $1555.51 amount of the judgment enjoined in the case of the Bank of Kentucky v. Theophilus Freeman No. 150 on the records of the court together with 20% damages on said sum $155, special damages for attorneys' fees, $226.62 costs incurred in keeping the slaves and costs of suit."

50. Connor v. Schneider, No. 5826, Fifth District Court of New Orleans, New Orleans, June 1874. This was a civil dispute in which Sarah Connor accused a tenant of owing her several months' unpaid rent.

51. Connor, f.w.c. v. The Bank of Kentucky, No. 1704, Fourth District Court of New Orleans, New Orleans, April 1848.

52. The US censuses of 1860 and 1870 indicate that Sarah Connor and Smith Isard lived together for at least a decade. See the following entries: *Eighth Census of the United States, 1860*, Dwelling 1074, Household 1044, Fourth Ward, Orleans Parish, New Orleans; *Ninth Census of the United States, 1870*, Dwelling 816, Household 1353, Third Ward, Orleans Parish, New Orleans.

53. "The Last of Sarah Conner's Case," *Daily Delta* (New Orleans), July 11, 1852. The article indicates that Freeman attempted to seize Connor as his slave after she was convicted of perjury. Did he hope to prevent her from being sent to prison? Was his aim to actually claim her as his enslaved property? We cannot know. His attempt does, however, reflect his lasting influence over Connor. Records from the US census indicate that Connor and Freeman continued to live together until at least 1850. See the following entry: *Seventh Census of the United States, 1850*, Dwelling 1426, Household 1787, Third Representative District, Orleans Parish, New Orleans.

54. Sarah Ann Connor registered her will with the District of Columbia on December 5, 1891, and her will is housed at the District of Columbia Archives. In her will, Sarah was explicit regarding her burial, writing the following: "At my death, I direct that my body shall be embalmed and thereafter placed in a casket lined with copper, and transported to New Orleans, Louisiana where it shall be placed in the outside steel casket I have ordered made for that purpose, and deposited in my tomb situate on lot numbered one hundred and eighty one (181) on Live Oak Avenue, in 'Cypress Grove Cemetery,' in the said City of New Orleans, there to rest until the day of judgment."

Conclusion

1. Toni Morrison, *The Source of Self-Regard: Selected Essays, Speeches, and Meditations* (New York: Vintage Books, 2019), 73.